Open Innovation in Action

How to be strategic in the search for new sources of value

Published by H-I Network
32 Duke Street
St James
London SW1Y 6DF
www.h-i.com

Tel: +44 (0)20 7747 2100
Fax: +44 (0)20 7747 7801
E-mail: research@h-i.com

Conditions of sale

First edition: October 2006

Printed in the United Kingdom

ISBN: 978-0-9551117-1-6

Contents

Part 1 – Introducing open innovation

Part 2 – The Five Ps: your checklist for holistic innovation

Part 3 – Case studies

Figures

Author profile

Andrew Gaule is the founder of the H-I Network (formerly the Henley Incubator), a thought-leadership forum comprised of senior executives from some of the world's leading organisations.

He is the creator of several popular management theories now in use at organisations such as Unilever, DHL, BOC and the Health Protection Agency:

- the "Five Ps", a methodology for ensuring innovation and venturing processes are sufficiently holistic and strategically aligned;

- the New Business Cube, a methodology for evaluating innovations throughout their development, from a holistic perspective, to prevent wastage and maximise the chances of successful deployment;

- the extrapreneur® terminology, a set of criteria used to identify individuals with an external perspective and the extra skills needed to develop ideas successfully in open innovation environments.

Andrew has been a co-author on many H-I Network reports, including: *Corporate Venturing; Rewarding Entrepreneurial Talent; Innovation Performance Measurement: Striking the Right Balance*; and *A Review of Leading Global Corporate Venture Units*.

He has been a senior executive in an IT services company and a business-change and project manager. He was previously an international SAP project manager and commercial manager with Unilever where he managed major divisional reorganisations and IT projects.

Andrew has an economics degree from St John's College, Cambridge, is a qualified chartered management accountant and gained his MBA at Henley Management College.

Acknowledgements

With thanks to:

Paul Tyrrell, who has provided the greatest support in consolidating and editing my thoughts.

P&G, QinetiQ, Shell, DSM and Tate & Lyle, for their case studies and suggestions.

QinetiQ, who sponsored our tailored-programme survey and provided a sounding board for many ideas.

Lisa Curteis, the team at Corven Consulting and the members of the H-I Network, for their help in building on previous reports, meetings and projects.

My wife Marie and daughter Mia for their support and inspiration.

Preface

How innovative is your company? If your answer isn't "very" then the chances are you are losing competitive advantage in your industry. In the globalised Knowledge Economy, the companies with the strongest growth are those who know how to corral good ideas and commercialise them rapidly. To survive, let alone thrive, you need to keep pace with the many technological and social trends currently accelerating and reinforcing one another worldwide.

Increased computing power; advances in telecommunications and networking technology; offshoring; lean manufacturing; smart logistics; trade liberalisation and harmonisation. All these things have made it cheaper and easier to take an idea from its point of

Consumers are more promiscuous and more discriminating than ever before

conception to its point of sale. As a consequence, smaller companies are now often in a better position than big rivals to pursue market niches, or even to disrupt whole sectors. At the same time, the behaviour of consumers is changing radically. The deluge of information now available to them via the Internet and other means has made them more discriminating and more promiscuous, simultaneously. If you fail to diversify your product or service portfolio adequately, they will readily go elsewhere.

You might think a sensible response to these trends would be to invest more in research and development, and thereby generate more and better ideas. This is certainly the strategy that many large companies have adopted in recent years. However, it is not enough to guarantee sustainable growth (at least, not without a broader strategy for generating value from the innovation process), for three main reasons:

1 Generating more and better ideas doesn't guarantee demand for those ideas, especially given today's surplus of products and services in so many industries.

2 It's no longer the case that vertically integrated organisations can claim to be more efficient than all their rivals in every stage of research, development and commercialisation. Those who try to keep everything in-house risk wasting money and passing on that waste to end-consumers in the form of higher prices.

3 It is now beyond the capabilities of any single organisation to monopolise the knowledge in its industry.

"Open innovation" could be the antidote to all these problems. If you've heard the term before then you will probably also be aware that it is being implemented by a growing number of leading organisations. In essence, it holds that ideas should be allowed to flow to where they can be most efficiently researched, developed and commercialised, regardless of where they originated, thereby generating maximum value for all the organisations involved.

However, our research and experience working with leading organisations has shown us that the basic open innovation theory – as defined in 2003 by Professor Henry Chesbrough of the University of California at Berkeley – needs to be extended to address several issues vital to a sustainable innovation process. For example:

- If an innovation process is to be maximally efficient then it needs to be based on "market pull" as well as "technology push". Too many companies still focus on the number of ideas they can generate, rather than the number of markets they can serve, and thereby waste money on products and services for which there is ultimately no demand.

- Similarly, the process must provide a strategic context for each innovation that flows through it, based on the overarching vision of the organisation. Too many organisations treat innovation as a bolt-on initiative rather than an integral part of their overall vision. As a result, they confuse and demoralise staff, divert resources to digressive ventures and ultimately dilute their core strengths. They also tend to try to adapt their strategy to great new ideas as they arise, rather than making sure they have a vision that defines what they should be focusing on in the first place.

Open innovation aids R&D processes by helping them to capture "false negatives", ideas that seem initially to offer no value but that later turn out to be profitable. It also helps to accelerate ideas in two ways: (i) by allowing them, at different stages of their development, to flow to different organisations where they can be handled at top speed; and (ii) by directing resources towards the most appropriate ideas and away from those that are unpromising or that could be more profitably exploited through licensing or divestiture.

In our view, the ideal open innovation system resembles a

Innovation should not be treated as a bolt-on initiative but as a key part of your strategy

beehive. A queen bee depends on worker bees and scouts to develop an accurate picture of the external environment while overseeing construction of the hive. Similarly, a chief executive may have no time to grasp the many external factors influencing the future of his or her organisation. Indeed, as you will learn in Chapter 1.2, "Technology Scouts" are a key part of the open innovation efforts of many leading companies.

A queen bee may face questions such as: "Where is the best source of nectar under the present circumstances?" or "If one plant is going out of season, should I shift my search for new food sources to another species?" Similarly, a chief executive must continually ask him or herself the question: "Are my markets changing to the point where I should shift resources into new lines of business?" There may even come a time when the entire hive has to be moved to ensure the survival of the swarm, analogous to the emergence of "disruptive technology" that renders traditional core markets obsolete.

The key to success under all these circumstances is communication. When bees find a new source of nectar they communicate the discovery to their queen and to other bees via a complex series of movements known as the "waggledance". In this book you'll learn methods of communication that can be carried out in an organisational context, so that senior executives are alerted to new sources of value and have all the information necessary to put the pursuit of that value in a strategic context.

In Part I we explain the origins and basic tenets of open innovation, and how we believe the theory should be extended based on insights from leading organisations – from the acceleration of innovation processes using external partnerships to the need for end-market awareness in even the most early concept stages.

In Part II we suggest five key criteria on which to develop an open innovation strategy – the Five Ps of "purpose, process, people, partners and performance." This is our basis for holistic thinking and strategic communication across the organisation.

And in Part III we examine how open innovation is being practised at five leading global companies. These case studies are the product of in-depth interviews with senior executives responsible for innovation at the following companies:

- **Procter & Gamble,** which has set itself the target of sourcing 50% of its innovations from outside the company;

- **QinetiQ,** where end-market research is helping to add value to early-stage research propositions;

- **Shell,** where the "GameChanger" initiative is identifying radical new technologies with very long-term potential;

- **DSM,** where open industrial parks and the identification of emerging business areas are helping to concentrate innovation resources for maximum effect;

- **Tate & Lyle,** where the shift from commodities to added-value products and services is being driven by open innovation principles.

Overall, this book is ideally suited to any manager who:

- feels they need to improve the innovation processes of their organisation but isn't sure how to go about it;

- is currently running an innovation process but isn't fully confident that they're thinking about it in a holistic way;

- understands their short-term priorities for innovation but isn't sure about how to prepare for the long-term; or

- wishes to benchmark their own innovation efforts against those of leading innovators.

Andrew Gaule
The H-I Network
London
October 2006

Part 1: Introducing open innovation

In this part of the book you will learn:

- why the "closed innovation" paradigm of knowledge-hoarding and vertical integration is changing;

- where the term "open innovation" originated and what it means;

- why allowing ideas to flow freely in and out of your organisation can accelerate your research, development and commercialisation processes, among many other benefits;

- which sources of fresh innovations are now preferred by leading companies, and which adhere best to open innovation principles;

- why it's important to consider potential markets during the early stages of an innovation's development, and continuously thereafter;

- where opportunities for open innovation are greatest in a typical supply chain, and the implications of this for different types of organisation.

1.1 The changing face of innovation

Ideas are the most valuable commodity in the Knowledge Economy. It's a mantra that Western companies are repeating louder than ever as they scramble to justify their premiums over low-cost rivals in Asia. Yet the best way to realise the commercial potential of an idea is not necessarily to keep it a secret. To become a true innovation – that is, something with an applied benefit rather than just a novel property – it needs to be supported by the right business model. And that's something the originating company may be unable to provide.

The key question to ask of any idea, whether it trickles up from your research team via e-mail or strikes you as you lower yourself into the bath, is: "Where can it be most fruitfully exploited?" You wouldn't keep a

Why keep an idea in-house if someone else is in a better position to commercialise it?

business function in-house if you could achieve a better balance of quality and cost outside; the globalisation of outsourcing has made it irresponsible to think otherwise. So why would you keep an idea in-house, if someone else were in a better position to commercialise it? Increasingly, companies are realising they can make more money from ideas via licensing arrangements, joint ventures and other means than by hoarding them for future development. They are also realising that by ridding themselves of the traditional "not invented here" attitude they can leverage the ideas, intellectual property (IP) and capabilities of other organisations, and thereby generate more value from in-house strengths.

Certainly, you'll make no money at all from an idea while it gathers dust on a shelf in your research department, or in the filing cabinet your lawyer uses for intellectual property rights (IPR). And if it ever ends up in such a static repository, you'll probably lose the opportunity to commercialise it altogether. Today's knowledge-workers are so mobile, and have such ready access to venture capital (VC), that they can easily take unused ideas to rivals or to start-up companies of their own. What's more, the burgeoning amount of knowledge available to business – via the Internet, the increasingly industry-oriented faculties of major universities and other sources – is

Sit on an idea and you're likely to have it stolen, duplicated or rendered obsolete

making it more likely that different companies will come up with the same idea simultaneously.

Yes, a patent will enable you to protect certain ideas under certain circumstances, but not without substantial resources to back it up. And it may do nothing more than stymie the efforts of your rivals. The practice of reverse-engineering new products as soon as they are launched, to determine how they can be imitated without infringing the inventor's IPR, is now well-established – indeed, it's a significant factor in the diminishing of product lifecycles. A growing number of companies also have the attitude that some kind of infringement is unavoidable given the complexity of modern technology, and that resulting disputes are simply a hazard of doing business, to be mopped up via patent trading or the courts. The bottom line is this: if you sit on an idea, you're likely to have it stolen, duplicated or rendered obsolete long before you develop the competences and capabilities needed to unlock its true value.

Of course, your company is not the only one facing such issues, and it follows that you may be best-placed to commercialise the surplus ideas of others. Indeed, you may be able to make a decent margin on ideas from a variety of sources – research institutions, suppliers, even customers. Many leading companies have proven in recent decades that you can in fact buy the majority of your innovations from external sources. In doing so, they have acknowledged that no single research and development (R&D) team can ever again hope to monopolise the knowledge of a particular industry. The new remit of R&D is to assess both internal and external ideas, and to work out how value can be extracted from the most promising.

Increasingly, the competitive advantage of companies will depend on how well they can create fresh revenue streams from their internal ideas and leverage their unique strengths to create margins from external ideas. Moreover, in industries where innovative activity seems to have reached a plateau, or where complexity is putting new products and services beyond the capabilities of single players, companies will need to be increasingly open and collaborative, even going so far as to work with direct rivals.

In other words, the "opening" of innovation is a trend that will bring major benefits to companies that grasp and exploit it early, and major problems to those too paranoid or short-sighted to follow suit.

Why closed innovation is doomed

For most of the 20th Century, leading companies benefited from a "virtuous circle" of investment in innovation. They recruited the best minds by offering unbeatable remuneration packages and facilities. They therefore made more breakthrough discoveries and brought more products and services to market than their rivals. In turn, they were able to pump more money back into R&D.

In many industries, proprietary knowledge and sales grew in parallel. The massive cost of setting up a competitive R&D function became a barrier to entry for small and medium-sized companies. Equally, the massive cost of maintaining such a function led industry leaders to become experts in vertical integration. In order to develop their increasingly complex ideas from start to finish – that is, from concept to commercialisation – they had to develop their competences and capabilities in everything from materials and tools to after-sales service and support.

This paradigm gave birth to multi-disciplinary giants such as Procter & Gamble (P&G), General Electric and 3M. It was also a factor in the development of "innovation factories" such as Bell Laboratories and

> # No single organisation can now sustain a knowledge monopoly in any particular industry

the Xerox Palo Alto Research Center (PARC). However, it has become virtually impossible for a single organisation to sustain a knowledge monopoly in any particular industry, owing to the following parallel trends:

● **Advances in information and communications technology**

The Internet is the ultimate force in the democratisation of knowledge. It makes such a high-volume of high-quality information available – most of it at a very low costs – that innovation has become easier at companies of all sizes. At one end of the product lifecycle, it has made research quicker, cheaper and easier. At the other, it has done the same for marketing, fulfilment and after-sales service. In between, it has become a benchmarking tool for products and services, and the basis for many valuable new processes.

The next big innovation could now arise just as easily in the bedroom of a young freelance electronics engineer in Shanghai as it could from the vast electronics laboratory of a processor manufacturer in Silicon Valley. In this context, large companies must draw strength from their unique capabilities: the priority is no longer to beat the solitary innovator to his discovery, but to find him and leverage his knowledge as quickly as possible afterwards.

Of course, the Internet is only the latest stage in the erosion of corporate knowledge silos. The telephone, the mobile phone, even physical communications such as cheap air travel – all these things have made it easier for innovations to arise elsewhere, and to proliferate beyond corporate control. As they continue to advance, so the impulse to hoard knowledge will become increasingly meaningless.

● **The mobility of the modern worker**

Higher education expanded massively in the West during the 20th Century, effectively reducing the cost of putting together a team of thinkers. As the rights of women and ethnic minorities improved, so they too added to the talent pool. The rise of the service industries made knowledge-work the ambition of most graduates. Brainpower became an abundant resource.

At the same time, competition for the best minds increased. The headhunting profession boomed, especially in fast-growing industries such as IT, where innovation was most vital to competitive advantage. Talented young professionals grew to expect a bidding war for their services. Indeed, they became so mobile in cities such as New York and London that they were given their own nickname, "Yuppies" (young and upwardly mobile). Companies began to generate innovations by stealing talent from their rivals or hiring it from the burgeoning consultancy sector.

By 1997, the US firm McKinsey – itself a leading consultancy – was predicting a "War For Talent". In the short-term, it predicted a global economy awash with ready capital in which ideas could be developed at the drop of a hat and workers were willing, as well as able, to change jobs frequently. In the medium to long-term, it predicted a skills shortage in the West as the proportion of young workers to old dependants sunk dramatically.

Does any of this sound familiar? It should do. Since that report was published we have experienced successive booms in IT, outsourcing, offshoring and, cyclically, mergers and acquisitions (M&A). Displacement has become a natural condition of the Western worker. Indeed, the best innovators in the globalised Knowledge Economy are likely to be those with a broad range of experiences under their belt – the ones who have travelled extensively and immersed themselves in other cultures, rather than sequestering themselves in the same laboratory for 20 years.

Of course a young professional who is both mobile and innovative is also likely to be a savvy player in the modern job market and therefore expensive to recruit. It is beyond the means of most companies to corral such people in significant numbers. Knowledge has therefore spilled out of the old corporate silos. Small, dynamic companies can offer them a more enjoyable and exciting lifestyle. And, increasingly, they can offer them great compensation too, especially among the numerous start-ups clustered around high-tech industries.

The rise of VC means innovative employees are more tempted than ever by start-ups

● **The growth of venture capital**

Since its emergence in the 1980s, the venture capital (VC) industry has permanently broken the "virtuous circle" of R&D investment described above. When knowledge leaks from a company these days – either because an innovative member of staff has left or because an idea left "on the shelf" has been mimicked – its destination is often a VC-backed start-up. There, an innovator will probably be rewarded with generous shareholdings, options and a leadership position they could never have achieved under their previous employer. They will also benefit from the unique freedoms and dynamism of a small-company environment.

Recent research led by Dr Rajshree Agarwal at the University of Illinois at Urbana-Champaign showed that, between 1977 and 1997, 25% of new entrants to the disk drive industry were started by individuals leaving larger companies in the same sector[1]. Today, most large companies in high-tech industries are inured to the idea that their most innovative employees will be tempted to set up rival businesses that are smaller and more nimble. At the same time, they are realising that the solution may have as much to do with recognition as remuneration. Creating structures and processes to retain and nurture innovators in-house is essential to any open innovation initiative, and we'll be returning to these issues in Part 2.

● The rising quality of suppliers

In the first half of the 20th Century, large companies didn't really need any help from small companies except in matters of distribution or highly specialised work. In the second half, they increasingly found that smaller companies could do certain things much better than they could, and for less money. The aforementioned trends were making it cheaper for small players to enter previously impenetrable markets. Meanwhile, the vertical integration model was spreading the resources of the big players too thinly.

As large companies sought to avoid duplicating their efforts, they began to outsource non-core business functions to independent specialists. As globalisation gathered speed and communications technology continued to advance, so it became natural to look worldwide for similar opportunities. Increasingly, large companies are outsourcing all but a handful of functions – those responsible for strategy, brand management and other core administrative responsibilities. The benefits of such disaggregation include optimal efficiency and flexibility; the drawbacks include an utter dependence on innovation competences and capabilities.

Brands are increasingly looking to their suppliers as sources of innovation

A related trend is that brands are looking to their suppliers as sources of innovation. Increasingly, the competitiveness of a brand depends on the efficiencies it can create along the chain of companies that support it – for example, Wal-mart, the giant US supermarket chain, has rolled out a radio-frequency identity tag standard across its network of suppliers. It follows that a beneficial new process could arise anywhere in the chain, and that there should be a mechanism in place to disseminate the use of that process upward and downwards as necessary. Equally, a materials supplier to, say, a consumer electronics brand is likely to innovate in ways that could significantly improve the properties of devices fashioned from its products.

Of course, such a supplier could easily inform another client of their discovery. They could even try to develop their brand strength to the point where they feel ready to market products and services themselves. Certainly, an increasing number of Asian companies have these ambitions, and do not see themselves merely as the low-cost adjuncts of uniquely creative brands in the West.

If you want to persuade a supplier that you are best-placed to exploit their discoveries fruitfully then you need the right incentives, communication policies and guiding principles of collaboration. As we'll discuss in Chapter 3.1, Procter & Gamble, the fast-moving consumer goods manufacturer, has developed a secure IT platform that enables it to share technology briefs with suppliers. Through this platform, it expresses specific needs openly – for example, "How can we make detergent perfume last longer after clothes come out of the dryer?" It then enables suppliers to reply privately, and to compete for the right to solve the problem in question.

This kind of openness is becoming increasingly necessary for another reason: in some industries, innovation has reached a near-plateau beyond which the only real growth will come from collaboration. You can only bolt small ideas onto big ones for so long: sooner or later you need a new platform for growth, and it may require you to form partnerships that previously seemed unlikely. Equally, in industries such as biotechnology and defence, where the technology is cutting-edge and commercialisation processes are hugely expensive, it may be financially unviable for companies to try innovating alone.

Open innovation comes of age

The term "open innovation" was coined by Professor Henry Chesbrough of the University of California at Berkeley, to describe the principles companies should follow if they wished to exploit the trends described above. He argued that in an ideal open innovation system, information about a particular idea would be allowed to flow in and out of the originating company at any stage of that idea's research and development.

In his seminal 2003 book, *Open Innovation: The New Imperative for Creating and Profiting from Technology*, Professor Chesbrough encapsulated the ethos of open innovation succinctly by explaining that it "combines internal and external ideas into architectures and systems whose requirements are defined by a business model."[2].

Figure 1, overleaf, details how Chesbrough compared the prevailing attitudes in closed and open innovation systems. In the following chapters, you'll learn how these translate into practical initiatives. However, it's vital in the first instance to understand where Chesbrough's model is crucial to your innovation process and where, based on our research and advisory experience, further measures are necessary to ensure the process is aligned to your overall strategy.

Many companies have embraced ideas in recent years that form part of the open innovation ideal: spin-off companies, for example, are increasingly the result of so-called intrapreneurial initiatives that cannot thrive within the structure or business model of the innovating organisation; and many companies have begun to license redundant IP where previously they would have stockpiled it. However, most still find full "openness" to be counter-intuitive, and are therefore failing to take the holistic and integrated approach that promises to give them the greatest competitive advantage.

Does your company contain "islands of expertise" that don't communicate? The danger of a piecemeal approach to open innovation, especially when it lacks an overriding vision, is that you simply create another island. Your "Skunkworks" R&D laboratory may do fantastic science, but unless it has clear objectives and a pervasive ability to spot commercial ideas then it may simply create resentment in other departments, and little value for the company as a whole. The need for communication in all directions, and

Figure 1: The contrasting principles of closed and open innovation

Closed

- The smart people in our field work for us.
- To profit from R&D, we must discover it, develop it and ship it ourselves.
- If we discover it ourselves, we will get it to market first.
- The company that gets an innovation to market first will win.
- If you create the most and the best ideas in the industry, you will win.
- We should control our IP, so that our competitors don't profit from our ideas.

Open

- Not all of the smart people work for us. We need to work with smart people inside and outside our company.
- External R&D can create significant value; internal R&D is needed to claim some portion of that value.
- We don't have to originate the research in order to profit from it.
- Building a better business model is better than getting to market first.
- If you make the best use of internal and external ideas, you will win.
- We should profit from others' use of our IP, and we should buy others' IP whenever it advances our own business model.

Source: *Open Innovation* (Harvard Business School Press, 2003), by Professor Henry Chesbrough.

between all departments, across open innovation networks is an issue we'll be returning to in Part 2.

Being more open doesn't mean exposing your organisation to overwhelming threats (at least, not if it is a carefully managed process); it simply means adapting to a world in which intellectual protectionism is much more challenging. Ultimately, the best reason to embrace open innovation fully may be that your rivals are planning to do so. Its aim is not simply to generate more ideas but to make sure you avoid wasting your money on the wrong ones, and instead pick the right ones to keep, share or sell. The sooner you can benefit from the resulting efficiencies, the greater your competitive advantage will be.

Being more open doesn't mean exposing your organisation to overwhelming threats

1.2 The benefits of being more open

Many corporate innovation processes can be illustrated as a funnel in which the bowl represents research and the spout represents development (see Figure 2). During the first stage, the vast majority of ideas a company receives in concept form are rejected as they prove to be less impressive than they seemed, in use elsewhere, based on false premises and so on. During the second stage, the remainder are gradually rejected because they prove to be inefficient to produce at scale, unappealing to their target market or rendered unviable by external factors.

The sides of the funnel represent the boundaries of the company, and where closed innovation is practised these boundaries are solid. The only value created by the innovation process at such a company comes from products and services that make it all the way through. By contrast, where open innovation is practised, the same boundaries are porous – that is, they allow knowledge to flow in and out of the company at any point during the R&D process. Company policy dictates what kind of knowledge can flow in which direction, and under what circumstances.

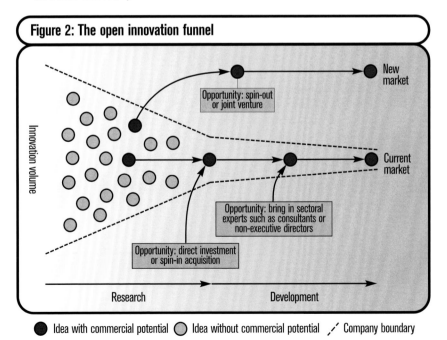

Figure 2: The open innovation funnel

Innovation volume

Opportunity: spin-out or joint venture

New market

Current market

Opportunity: bring in sectoral experts such as consultants or non-executive directors

Opportunity: direct investment or spin-in acquisition

Research   Development

● Idea with commercial potential ○ Idea without commercial potential ⟋ Company boundary

For example, while researching an idea you may realise that:

- you'd make more money by licensing it to an external organisation than by developing and commercialising it yourself;

- its development could be more efficiently carried out elsewhere, making it cost-effective to enlist the help of an external organisation in return for a share of the eventual profits in any future business the idea helps to create; or

- you could buy a similar idea from outside the company that would be cheaper to develop and/or more effective.

Similarly, while developing an idea you may realise that:

- its commercialisation would be accelerated and/or its business model would be enhanced if you formed a partnership with an external organisation for technical or distribution help, or other reasons;

- although there is a compelling case for keeping it in-house to the point of commercialisation, it is beyond your capabilities to develop it fully, meaning the recruitment of a sectoral expert or specialised non-executive director could be required to help manage things;

- you simply don't have the capacity to commercialise it, in which case it may make sense to divest the whole venture; or

- you feel it is strong enough, and sufficiently far removed from your core business, to merit its own profit centre or spin-off company.

The last of these situations is especially likely when the idea in question is potentially disruptive, i.e. capable of changing a market sector or industry fundamentally. The business model of such an idea is likely to be so different from that of your core offerings that, to develop successfully, it requires its own budget, corporate structure and even premises. Why should you research or develop an idea that could cannibalise your existing markets? That's the question your incumbent R&D department will be asking if you try to keep a disruptive idea in-house, especially if your scientists and engineers have any kind of incentive scheme linked to the eventual commercial performance of their ideas.

When a little-known inventor called James Dyson pitched his idea for a bagless vacuum cleaner to the world's leading manufacturers of household cleaning appliances in the 1980s, he was laughed out of the room. The market in replacement bags was huge, and the last thing the manufacturers wanted to do was support an idea that could disrupt it. None had enough foresight to imagine that the man in front of them would eventually develop his idea alone and thereby seriously erode their markets.

Open innovation should stop you from rejecting smash-hit ideas that initially look valueless

If those manufacturers had practised open innovation at the time they met Mr Dyson, the flow of knowledge through their companies may have enabled them to predict the emergence of the bag-less vacuum cleaner, and persuaded them to get in on the act as quickly as possible. Equally, as we shall discuss below, they may have been able to take an option in Mr Dyson's business without committing themselves to a defensive, and expensive, R&D programme.

Open innovation helps to prevent such "false negatives" – that is, it makes it less likely for companies to reject ideas that look valueless or value-destroying initially but that later turn out to be smash hits.

If a little-known inventor knocked on the door of your office today, clutching a potentially disruptive idea, would you have the people and procedures in place to spot and seize the value in that idea? Increasingly, large companies are trying to welcome innovators more warmly. At the same time, they are actively looking for ideas originating beyond their walls – often with the collaboration of other organisations – with a view to investing in ideas or "spinning them in" to their own R&D functions. The main search methods they are using are as follows:

Technology scouts

Technology scouts are typically senior members of R&D staff, with a talent for spotting the applied benefits of emerging technologies and the business sense to understand how such technologies could be exploited commercially. Their job descriptions include a remit to search for innovations outside the company, whether by attending trade shows, meeting entrepreneurs or simply spotting underexploited products on the shelves of foreign convenience stores (see Chapter 3.1 for details of how Procter & Gamble uses technology scouts). A specific proportion of their time is dedicated to this search, and they may be given the opportunity to lead the research and development of any valuable idea they find.

To be effective, a scout must regard their external-facing perspective as a duty. Otherwise their instinct may be to protect their traditional turf. A recent survey by QinetiQ, the defence technology company – where spinning ideas into other organisations is a major revenue stream – found that companies without scouts tend to have R&D departments that feel threatened by good ideas pitched from outside. A good scout acts as a point of access for good ideas, especially if those ideas have the potential to be disruptive. In most companies, innovation is not often talked about at the level of industries, market sectors, or even brands and concepts. Usually, it takes the form of low-risk, incremental enhancements to existing products and services. The scout should provide a broader, more open perspective.

University collaboration

If you want to be innovative, you have to collaborate with universities at some level. They're the talent pools from which you'll draw your future recruits, and from which you can draw individual experts or teams on a temporary basis, to help you with specific R&D tasks. They carry out some of the latest research in every industry, in a multi-disciplinary environment that encourages the cross-fertilisation of ideas. And increasingly they are sources of ideas that are ripe for commercialisation.

Leading universities have become much more sophisticated in recent years at licensing IP, forming joint ventures with private-sector companies and, to a limited extent, setting up spin-off companies of their own. Stanford University, for example, grossed $384m in licensing royalties in 2004-05; in the same year, it also made around $336m from the flotation of Google, because it backed early development of the search engine under former students Larry Page and Sergey Brin. However, the new breed of IP commercialisation or "technology transfer" departments at universities across the West has yet to mature, and many companies still find the process of licensing IP from universities to be a frustrating experience.

In the UK, for example, the government has recently provided money to universities to enable them to commercialise more of their IP and thereby, in theory, generate their own revenue streams. However, few technology transfer departments here are able, at present, to cover their own costs. And along with their counterparts across Europe they tend to try extracting value from ideas via start-ups when, critics argue, they may be able to extract more via licensing deals. A recent study by the Milken Institute, a US think-tank, found that universities in Europe establish three times as many companies relative to research expenditures in biotechnology as those in North America[3]. A related problem is the funding gap between university commercialisation efforts and market expectations of development-ready ideas. Typically, start-ups backed by UK universities don't have the resources to commercialise products and services without development partners, yet they lack the money to prove their concepts in a way that would win them those partners – today's market for professional advice means it can cost £25k to put together a proposal in order to get £1m funding.

Many companies still regard investing in university IP as onerous and risky

Furthermore, academic inventors tend to over-estimate the commercial value of their ideas. They typically feel the value of their IP is equivalent to 80% of any resulting business, while potential investors typically feel it is worth around 15%, given the significant costs and risks of development. Overall, many companies still regard investing in university IP as onerous and risky, making it vital for advocates of open innovation to develop effective engagement models.

Another form of collaborative arrangement between companies and universities that is growing in popularity is the corporate sponsorship of facilities, departments or even faculties. For example, the Unilever Centre for Molecular Science Informatics at Cambridge University has been open since October 2000, and now employs about 40 scientists, who dedicate some of their time to their sponsor in return for world-class facilities. Similarly, Rolls-Royce has built around 25 "university technology centres" since 1990 – from Oxford in the UK to Pusan in South Korea – in which its investment in facilities buys access to engineering students for work on specific R&D projects.

Such facilities are potentially very valuable sources of innovation, as well as R&D support, in the sense that any ideas they develop on the sponsor's time should become the sponsor's IP. A key consideration for any company considering such a collaborative venture is obviously the balance between proximity and specialty; that is, you need to trade off your ease of commu-

If universities are such hotbeds of innovation then why not build your own?

nication with the institution against its level of thought-leadership in your industry.

Tate & Lyle, the food and industrial ingredients manufacturer whose open innovation efforts are described in more detail in Chapter 3.5, spends 12% of its R&D budget on "alliances with academic institutions", and has concentrated much of this spending on a handful of universities in the mid-Western US near some of its major facilities. For example, it has invested several hundred thousand dollars in Purdue University, Indiana, which is situated near two Tate & Lyle corn-processing plants. The university, which has a reputation for leading agricultural research, has used the money to set up a food carbohydrate laboratory and to part-fund its "Whistler Center for Carbohydrate Research". Part of the return on this investment for Tate & Lyle is the secondment of around 60 of Purdue's graduate students to positions in chemistry, engineering and other areas.

Open R&D campuses

If universities are such hotbeds of innovation then why not build your own? Many companies have done exactly this over the past few decades, at least in microcosm, in the form of dedicated R&D parks. Initially, these campuses mimicked the collegiate style of real universities, in an effort to stimulate innovation through the cross-fertilisation of ideas between disciplines. But they lacked the openness of real universities – that is, the willingness to allow knowledge to flow freely in and out.

Now many such campuses are transforming themselves based on open innovation principles. At its most basic level, this transformation can take the form of an invitation to external organisations from the governing company's supply chain or industry cluster to share the same space. The presence of a variety of organisations can be enough to lead to "interstitial innovation" as staff find it easier to communicate face-to-face. And the importance of socialising together shouldn't be discounted either – leading innovators regard communal canteens and other social areas as a crucial stimulant for new ideas, not to mention a way to get staff to extend their meetings outside of billable work hours.

A recent survey by the H-I Network found that, for a traditional R&D campus to transform itself successfully into an open innovation environment, the governing company must consider the following points:

- Partnering with specialist science-park developers and relevant local government bodies, such as the UK's regional development agencies (RDAs), is critical.

- The performance criteria for the campus should be different from those of the governing company, though strategic alignment is vital.

- Clear policies must exist to define acceptable tenants and acceptable behaviour from those tenants.

- Clusters of expertise and physical proximity requirements may vary between different industries. A campus dedicated to computer technology could, for example, reasonably be extended virtually to encourage collaboration on software projects.

Unilever, the fast-moving consumer goods company, undertook such a transformation in 2004 at its Colworth R&D campus in Bedfordshire, one of its main R&D sites. The key driver behind this process was globalisation: in all its markets, the company was experiencing increased time pressures, shortened product life cycles and stimulated business restructuring. As we shall discuss further below, open innovation offered a way to not only tap additional sources of innovation but also accelerate the development of new products. Unilever's plan to extend the Colworth site and open it to external organisations involved forging a 50:50 joint venture with Arlington Securities, a leading business park developer.

Other open R&D campuses include:

- **The High Tech Campus Eindhoven, the Netherlands**. This 220-acre site used to be the exclusive research laboratory complex of Royal Philips Electronics, with a working population of around 4,000 scientists and engineers. Then in 1999 it began to expand and invite other organisations to set up their own operations on-site. Specifically, Philips wanted its new tenants to be "R&D-oriented" high-tech companies, with specialties such as information and communications technology. The campus architecture uses open-plan designs, transparent walls and numerous informal meeting spaces to support open innovation. Over the coming years, the number of buildings on the site will rise to around 30, with a total surface area of more than 174,000m^2 and a working population of over 8,000.

- **Adastral Park, Suffolk, UK**. This 111-acre site used to be a military base. In 1975, it became a communications laboratory complex exclusive to British Telecom. Since the late 1990s it has become a second home to a variety of communications technology companies including Alcatel, Cisco and Fujitsu; and to educational institutions including University College, London and the University of Essex. The park, which is still owned and managed by BT, now has a working population of around 4,000.

Incubator units

Traditional R&D functions tend to treat each idea as one of many flowing through the company's innovation process. They can therefore fail to give the most promising ideas enough market-orientation to realise their maximum value. A corporate incubator, by contrast, treats promising ideas as discrete business units, with the aim of accelerating their commercialisation or developing them to the point where they can win backing from external venture capital funds. In an open innovation environment, it puts the emphasis on using partnerships with external organisations as a means to accelerate R&D.

At least, this is the theory. In reality, most corporate incubators have failed to produce innovations that serve their parent company's overall goals. The problem is that boards tend to regard innovation as an abstract discipline that cannot easily be aligned to strategy. When they decide to set up an incubator, they often think it is enough simply to put a group of talented people into a well-equipped room. As a result, they often fail to funnel the energies of that group sufficiently, and thereby waste time and resources.

These were among the findings of a 2005 study by Andrew Campbell and Robert Park of Ashridge Strategic Management Centre[4]. The same authors have since developed a tool called the "New Business Traffic Lights" to help managers formulate a strategic case for their innovations. You can find a brief description of the Traffic Lights in Chapter 2.1 of this book, and a detailed description, including examples of how the tool is being applied by leading organisations, in a previous H-I Network report, *Winning Ideas for Strategic Growth and Venturing*.

In the context of open innovation, strategic alignment becomes particularly important. An incubator should have the freedom to provide ideas with the most appropriate business model, even if that model has no precedent in the parent company. In theory, it is therefore the ideal setting in which to develop technologies that could disrupt the company's existing businesses in the short-term but provide a more substantial revenue stream in the medium- or long-term. By screening ideas thoroughly without imposing restrictions on how they should be commercialised, it should also help to prevent "false negative" rejections of good ideas. Ultimately, it should help promote a more open culture across the organisation.

The critical issue the parent company must consider is how close to keep the incubator to its incumbent R&D function. If it shares the same personnel and facilities then it is less likely to find and support ideas outside the company's core offerings. If it is too far removed then the company may find it duplicates its efforts, or that the businesses it produces are of insufficient scale or strategic alignment to be viable.

Corporate venture funds

A corporate venture fund operates in much the same way as any independent venture capital fund. It makes small investments in various ideas in the expectation that some will provide a mediocre return or none at all, while others will be very successful indeed. It generally makes investments in the same or related industries to that of its parent company, so that it can utilise the experience of the parent company to increase the value of its portfolio.

A corporate or indirect venture fund could help you hedge against future disruption

In the context of open innovation, it can also: alert the parent company to emerging technologies, thereby giving it a better sense of how industry trends will play out; improve the capabilities of the parent company by giving it access to the latest research findings and technological breakthroughs; and hedge against the possibility that the R&D function of the parent company is focusing on the wrong markets, by investing in start-ups that threaten to disrupt those markets in the medium- to long-term.

Consider Tate & Lyle again, for example. Its overriding strategic vision, which you can learn more about in Chapter 3.5 of this book, is to shift its focus from low-margin commodities to high-margin, "value-added" food ingredients and associated services. However, it has also recently announced a joint venture with DuPont to develop a substance known as Bio-PDO™, which effectively produces textiles from corn and has many other non-food-related applications. DuPont didn't have the necessary expertise and capabilities in fermentation and manufacturing to fulfil the commercial potential of this material alone, so in line with open innovation principles it decided to shared the idea.

The bigger potential problem is that, during the 10-15 years the venture will take to pay for itself, Bio-PDO™ could be rivalled by other technologies. Clearly, Tate & Lyle cannot mitigate against such a prospect simply by pouring more money into its R&D function. But what it can do is make strategic investments in similar technologies and potential rivals via its £25m Ventures fund. CEO Iain Ferguson has declared that he wants this fund to be as independent as possible, so that its long-term investment decisions cannot be distorted by its parent's short-term needs, and so that it can attract further funding from other sources of venture capital. In this way, it should act as an options box for Tate & Lyle in the future – a kind of innovation insurance policy. From a financial perspective, the fund is like any other from which the company might buy ideas, but from a strategic perspective it is aligned to Tate & Lyle's goals.

Indirect venture funds

Indirect venture funds enable companies to spread their bets even further when it comes to hedging against the possibility of disruption. Managed by independent investment houses, they back small companies in particular sectors using money from big companies in those sectors. So, for example, the NGEN Fund, based in Santa Barbara, California, specialises in materials and clean technology, with numerous corporate investors including Unilever, DuPont and DSM.

The benefit for the portfolio companies in this arrangement is that their ultimate investors validate their innovations, provide pertinent R&D advice and may eventually spin those innovations into their own operations. The benefit for the big incumbents, aside from hedging, is an improved understanding of the sectors in question. By investing in the fund they are in effect outsourcing some of the responsibility of identifying promising new trends in that sector. And they are buying hands-on experience of the latest innovations, while keeping abreast of start-ups.

Moreover, personnel can be regularly exchanged between these funds and their corporate investors. An R&D manager may be seconded to NGEN, for example, to provide the fund's financial experts with a relevant scientific or engineering perspective as they carry out due diligence. In return, he or she gets to see the fund's deal flow, and therefore gets even closer to the trends at play in the sector concerned.

Joint opportunities

Brainstorming between companies, even rivals, is becoming increasingly popular as a source of innovation. Now that most industries offer a surplus of products and services, and some have reached a plateau of quality, the most radical new innovations tend to be those that package numerous properties or functions. Accordingly, companies that explore the possibility of combining one another's ideas at the very beginning of the innovation process stand a better chance of inventing something valuable than those who remain closed until they can bring proven concepts to the table.

Brainstorming between companies is an increasingly popular source of innovation

Take the Senseo coffee brewing system, for example. This water-boiling gadget and its associated "pods" of coffee has met with the approval of over 10 million buyers worldwide, who use it to brew high-quality coffee as easily as a mug of instant granules. The system was conceived and developed by Philips, the electronics company, and Douwe Egberts, the Dutch coffee company owned by US consumer goods producer Sara Lee. Neither partner could have developed the system cost-effectively on its own, but each earns a margin from one element of the venture in which it can leverage its unique strengths.

If your company is considering a similar collaboration then you need to consider where you can bring your unique strengths to bear on the venture, and thereby extract the most value. In the case of Senseo, the division of responsibilities is obvious, but few collaborations are so clear-cut. Furthermore, you may need to work on the basis that the venture will be an independent company with its own financial and management structures. In this way, the venture should be better able to adapt to the rigours of its market, without being distorted by the influence of its parents.

Brainstorming sessions can give rise to traditional joint ventures, licences, customer/supplier relationships or other types of arrangement. Equally, they may simply stimulate innovative thinking among those in attendance thanks to a diverse guest list and an agenda focused on a particular future scenario. For example, the H-I Network regularly runs "Joint Opportunity Assemblies" in which senior executives from various industries discuss broad topics such as ageing populations, sustainable energy or health and wellness. In our experience, ideas originating at such events are only viable if they are "championed" by a particular individual. As we'll discuss more in Part 2, even the best ideas can wither on the vine unless they are supported by the right people.

IP repositories

Embracing open innovation fully means declaring what you know to anyone who might be interested. To this end, an increasing number of companies are setting up IP repositories that are accessible on-line to selected potential partners. Their chief aim is to encourage cross-licensing or patent-trading deals under which rivals can buy into their IP and thereby press ahead with complex designs that would otherwise constitute infringements. Accordingly, it is now best practice for companies to check the IP repositories of their rivals as a matter of course.

One of the biggest IP repositories in the world belongs to IBM, the US computer technology giant, which currently has about 40,000 active patents worldwide. In 1997, the company launched an internal initiative called the "Intellectual Property Network", and with it a searchable database of all IBM patents filed since 1971, available to the public via the Internet. In 2000, this Network was spun out of IBM to form a wholly independent company called Delphion, which would provide patent-search software and services. Delphion was later acquired by Thomson Corporation, the business and professional information provider. Meanwhile, IBM's "Virtual Innovation Center", accessible to registered partners via the IBM.com website, provides access to a raft of services including one-on-one development advice, systems architecture consultations in eight languages and even remote testing of systems using IBM components.

While repositories such as IBM's may provide a source of innovation for your company, you may find that setting up your own reduces the number of inappropriate or duplicate ideas brought to you by external innovators.

1.3 Surviving the innovation surplus

In the previous chapter we introduced the innovation funnel, a visual representation of the typical process during which a company chooses ideas to commercialise by a process of elimination. It's an illustration that has been widely embraced by most commentators on corporate innovation. However, it's not as static as many make out. Although the basic shape remains valid, it's proportions are changing.

Most companies are finding that the bowl of the funnel is widening. Why? Because the sheer amount of knowledge available to them has increased exponentially in recent years, and the number of potential innovations they could consider has followed suit. Advances in information and communications technology, globalisation and other forces have all generated innovations faster than companies can reasonably sort through them. Moreover, the convergence of technologies has created a new breed of innovation – nanotechnology, for example, only exists because of overlaps between physics, chemistry and biology. As these trends gather pace, the amount of R&D resources that companies can dedicate to each idea they

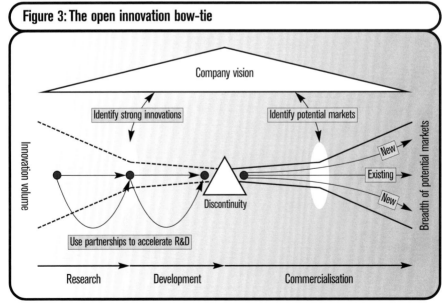

Figure 3: The open innovation bow-tie

come across is being reduced. In other words, the spout of the innovation funnel is narrowing.

In a closed innovation environment, this leads to a vicious cycle. Spend less on research and you are less likely to pick the right ideas for development. Spend less on development and you are less likely to retain the right ideas for commercialisation. Fewer new products or services means a reduced budget for R&D. This is what the commentators mean when they say the R&D functions of some companies have begun to lose their "critical mass".

Yet simply throwing more money at R&D isn't the answer. As we discussed above, one of the chief ways in which open innovation generates value is by making R&D functions more efficient. So the idea that companies should spend a certain proportion of their turnover on R&D – a benchmark still popular in many quarters – is largely bogus. A falling R&D expenditure as a percentage of sales could in fact be an indication that an open innovation programme is succeeding. And in any case, the only figure you shouldn't be trying to reduce as a percentage of sales is profit.

To reiterate, open innovation lets ideas flow to where they can be most efficiently handled at each stage of the commercialisation process, so that each player in that process can extract the maximum possible value. It is a "free trade" of ideas, managed through intellectual property rights, non-disclosure agreements and fair divisions of value between partners.

How to focus your innovation efforts

What the incumbent best-practice models of corporate innovation are lacking is a sense of market perspective. That's one of the strongest findings to emerge from our research and contact with innovators at major companies. As Figure 3 illustrates, the ideal process doesn't really look like a funnel at all. It looks like a bow-tie. To use open innovation effectively, your company must concentrate not only on the left-hand side of the bow-tie, where new technologies are emerging, but at the right-hand side, where new markets are possible.

If you can improve your knowledge at both ends of the bow-tie, then you can become more effective at identifying value-creation opportunities throughout the process. Thus, if a market need can be predicted far enough in advance then the need for a particular innovation can be identified.

Better still, a technology already in development can be steered so that its market appeal is redirected or broadened. In this context, the essential role of any large company becomes to create links between innovations and markets, no matter where that company extracts its value.

As open innovation proliferates, companies in business-to-business industries will need to improve their knowledge of the changing needs of end-consumers. Otherwise, they will lose competitive advantage to those who demonstrate the market potential of their offerings. Yet even companies that face consumers on a day-to-day basis shouldn't be complacent. In our experience, it is possible to lose perspective if you farm out too much research to marketing agencies.

Knowledge of end-customer needs is increasingly vital across supply chains

The area of "discontinuity" at the centre of Figure 3 represents the point at which you may have to make fundamental changes to your organisation. As we'll discuss further in Chapter 3.5, Tate & Lyle realised it needed to shift its focus from commodities to added-value products and services if it wanted to sustain its growth and competitive advantage, so it invested more in end-consumer research. It then responded to trends in the needs of end-consumers by concentrating its innovation resources on a handful of key areas such as nutraceuticals, and launched services to help clients incorporate ingredients in their products. However, the change wasn't just one of budgetary reallocation. It required major organisational restructuring – its sales people, for example, had to adapt from selling bulk commodities to specialised ingredients, based on a deeper understanding of end-consumers. Added-value business now accounts for half Tate & Lyle's profits even though it only accounts for around a quarter of its sales.

The danger of using only the first part of the funnel as your innovation model is that you miss the emergence of new markets and fundamental changes to your existing ones. Consider Kodak's slow reaction to the emergence of digital photography, for example. The company has now moved into diverse markets such as healthcare imaging, but for a long time its innovation efforts remained chemistry-based, rooted in analogue photography. As a result it had to slash its R&D staff from a few hundred to a few dozen. Chief executive Antonio Perez said recently that the company was in the "final stages" of a $3bn adjustment. But the company nevertheless made a net loss of $282m in the second quarter of 2006.

Towards an integrated innovation strategy

Practise closed innovation and you're responsible for every stage of the value-extraction process; practise open innovation and you need to concentrate on the stage in which you can extract the biggest slice of value.

During its first few years in the private sector, QinetiQ, the defence technology company, focused on research, because that had traditionally been its strength. However, this first stage of the idea commercialisation process was the one that had the lowest budgets. In a typical R&D process, 20% of the expenditure takes place in the research phase and 80% in the development phase. So, during the former, there was relatively little money available to QinetiQ from other large organisations. At the same time, the company worried that the innovations of its own creation, which it was attempting to license via a "technology push" strategy, were being undervalued.

Improved end-market awareness has helped QinetiQ boost licence values and sales leads

In recent years, QinetiQ has invested more in improving its awareness of end-customer needs and thereby strengthened its hand in licensing negotiations. Indeed, as Stephen Lake, the director of the company's New Business Accelerator team, points out in Chapter 3.2, greater end-market awareness has actually enabled it to generate more sales leads. Significantly, the far-left and far-right of the bow-tie represent phases of minimal capital outlay in the process of commercialising and idea. It makes sense for QinetiQ to leave the more capital-intensive phases to an external partner.

Of course, to make optimal use of external knowledge you need to provide that knowledge with clear routes in and out of your organisation, and be able to find similar paths through the structures of potential partners. It's in the nature of globally disaggregated organisations to have different departments with different areas of expertise based in different locations. So if, for example, you've got an innovation that could improve a complex piece of technology, how should you go about selling it to the developer of that technology? Should you go through a local office, a national office, the international headquarters, the divisional headquarters for the relevant business area, the group's intellectual property department or some other point of contact?

As the receiving company, you ideally need a single point of contact through which to accept unsolicited offers of partnerships, such as the single phone number for all enquiries to QinetiQ. Equally, you must have the mechanisms in place to channel ideas to the right person. It's not advisable to let a good idea arrive on the desk of a scientist or engineer who is in the process of developing a rival technology. The chances are, they'll feel threatened and will leave that idea gathering dust in their in-tray, no matter how good it is. Being open means being unafraid to have the potential of your internal R&D challenged.

Why every idea should be aligned with your strategic vision

The question of which innovations and which markets to focus on should be answered by the organisation's overarching strategy. The vision could be termed the "roof" that protects and contains the whole process. It should be developed in line with open innovation principles, in that it must be informed by knowledge from both ends of the bow-tie and be subject to iteration if markets change fundamentally. It must also be promoted continuously, throughout the organisation, from the board downwards. In the context of innovation, this should ensure that digressive ideas are culled, licensed or divested as soon as possible.

When innovations get stuck, it's often because their contribution to the overall strategic vision isn't recognised or understood. Frequently the leaders of innovation projects say, "We don't understand where we fit." They don't get the attention of the top people, they don't get enough "airtime" throughout the company and ultimately they don't get adequate resources. It's possible, of course, that the innovations in question are worthless. Or that they have the wrong people working on them. As we'll discuss in Chapter 2.3, a strong idea is unlikely to succeed unless it has a "champion" fully invested in it. However, imagining you will "learn by doing" is a sure-fire way to waste resources. Yes, progressing an innovation will always be an iterative process, and there are always failures along the way to success, but you're very unlikely to find a strategic reason for commercialising an idea in retrospect. Starting to innovate from a clearly defined area of strategic interest is far more efficient.

Where is open innovation easier?

Open innovation activity tends to be greater at the bottom of supply chains (see Figure 4). Why? Because here it takes only a simple deal structure to generate value from external knowledge. Imagine, for example, that a yarn manufacturer invents a particularly strong and light type of thread. By alerting textile manufacturers to the properties of that thread, it could stimulate the creation of new types of fabric, and thereby sell more yarn. In turn, the textile manufacturers could stimulate the creation of new types of apparel, and thereby sell more fabric.

In a closed innovation environment, the yarn and fabric manufacturers would market their new products on the basis of properties, performance, cost and so on. In an open innovation environment, they would exchange much more information with prospective clients. For example, they could suggest what the applied benefits of their products would be in each client's markets. By the same token, the clients could alert the suppliers to the changing demands of end-users. The underlying point here is that the stronger your relationship with other companies in your supply chain, and the more willing you are to exchange knowledge, the greater the potential income for everybody.

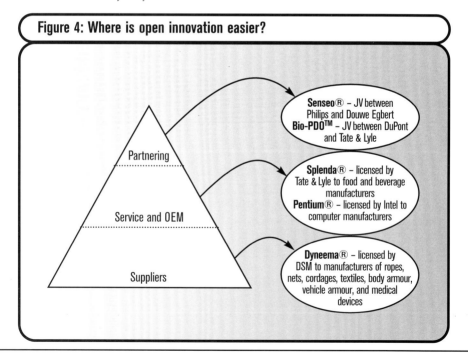

Figure 4: Where is open innovation easier?

Of course, here at the bottom of the supply chain, margins are lower, and most innovations are about lowering the cost of a material or component without lowering its performance. Further up, margins increase in inverse proportion to opportunities.

The next level is arguably that of enabling technologies such as advanced electronic components, food and pharmaceutical ingredients or software. Here, open innovation is governed by original-equipment-manufacturer (OEM), licensing or service-level agreements. So for example, Tate & Lyle manufacturers the sugar-substitute Splenda® and sells it to food and beverage manufacturers so that they can create diverse new products of their own. It also offers a raft of added-value services to help clients add the ingredient to their industrial processes and achieve specific taste, consistency or nutritional goals (see Chapter 3.5).

If your company is situated at this level then it probably already has the people it needs to benefit from open innovation of this sort – people who are used to forging OEM, licensing or service-level agreements. But are they clear about the strategic context for such deals? And have they leveraged as much internal and external knowledge as possible to envision the markets these deals will eventually tap? Again, it is in your interests to foster the exchange of ideas between those people and their counterparts in other organisations.

At the top of the supply chain, open innovation does occur between brand-owners, but it is much more difficult to manage. Here, partnership structures such as joint ventures or strategic alliances are crucial to the entire R&D process. The resulting ventures tend to involve complex and unprecedented business models, making it crucial that all parties understand their place in the value chain. Are you being saddled with phases where the potential margins are too low or the capital exposure is too high? Or are you able to extract just as much value from your responsibilities as your partners are from theirs? These are the kinds of questions you need to ask yourself before agreeing to such a venture.

Part 2: The Five Ps

In this part of the book you will learn how to put together an holistic, integrated innovation strategy. Many ideas make it part-way through an organisation's innovation process before their contribution to the overall strategy of the organisation is considered. The Five Ps prevent that from happening. They are five key considerations for the building and maintenance of an innovation strategy that is fully aligned to the overall strategy, rather than being treated as a mere adjunct to the organisation. They are:

- **Purpose.** A consideration of why you need to innovate and what type of innovation you need to practice.

- **Process.** A consideration of the development stages common to all innovation processes, plus helpful ancillary processes.

- **People.** A consideration of whether you have the human resources available to ensure innovations are supported in the right way at the right time.

- **Partners.** A consideration of external partners who may be able to help you accelerate the development of an innovation, unlock its value more easily or provide a destination for licensing deals and divestitures.

- **Performance.** A consideration of the performance criteria you need to attach to individual innovations and to the process as a whole.

2.1 Purpose

Why do you need to innovate? Notwithstanding the obvious pressures of the global Knowledge Economy, this is an important question to ask of your organisation if you want your innovation strategy to be holistic and integrated, not to mention aligned to your overall strategy. If you operate in the private sector then increasing shareholder value is clearly a key objective. If you operate in the public sector then you may set yourself the priority of maximising revenue so that resources can be redistributed. Beyond these things, you may face a variety of additional pressures to innovate in particular ways depending on the technological space in which you operate, the changing nature of your target markets, your regulatory environment and so on.

As we discussed in Chapter 1.3, the overall company vision is the primary lens through which to focus your innovation efforts. It may be subject to different industry cycles at different companies, but it should always reflect "three horizons" of growth, according to authors Mehrdad Baghai,

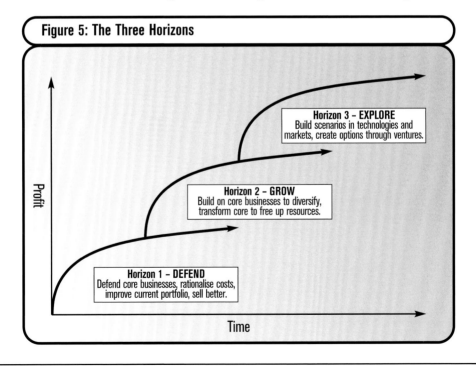

Figure 5: The Three Horizons

Horizon 3 – EXPLORE
Build scenarios in technologies and markets, create options through ventures.

Horizon 2 – GROW
Build on core businesses to diversify, transform core to free up resources.

Horizon 1 – DEFEND
Defend core businesses, rationalise costs, improve current portfolio, sell better.

Profit

Time

A balanced venture portfolio should flatten your innovation peaks and troughs

Stephen Coley and David White. This trio of McKinsey consultants introduced their Three Horizons model (see Figure 5) in their 2000 book, *The Alchemy of Growth*. The model illustrated the simple but powerful idea that, to achieve sustainable growth, a company has to consider three objectives: (i) defend core businesses, (ii) build new businesses; and (iii) explore options for future businesses.

Which of these areas does your company need to develop? That's what you have to ask yourself primarily, if you want a cohesive innovation strategy. It's no good focusing purely on the first horizon, or you'll see your growth collapse once your supply of fresh innovations has run out – often the case at companies with strong core businesses, who feel no urgency to innovate and therefore fail to spot disruptive technologies, such as bag-less vacuum cleaners or MP3 music singles.

Equally, you may find that focusing on the third horizon before fully exploiting the opportunities presented to you by the second is a waste of money. This was the experience of Shell when its "Internet Ventures" fund, launched in November 2000 to capitalise on the dotcom boom, suffered badly from the dotcom crash. The fund turned out to be way ahead of its time in terms of optioning ventures aligned to the overall company's long-term strategy, and Shell is now paying more attention to the diversification of its fuel range – a clear "second horizon" objective.

Towards the balanced venture portfolio

The Three Horizons model provides companies with useful rules of thumb for long-term planning, but we have found it is better to evaluate portfolios of innovation investments using a more advanced analysis, as illustrated in Figure 6. This grid, when populated with a company's various ventures, enables the company in question to visualise where all of its innovation investment is going, and thereby helps it to decide which ventures to keep, sell or share. In many cases it highlights wasteful ventures that have been allowed to tick over because their strategic fit hasn't been considered properly, or because the unique strengths of the company are unlikely to leverage much value from the innovation concerned, or because the ratio of fit to capability has been revealed as insufficiently attractive.

The higher the level of internal capability in relation to an idea, the better position you are in to extract value from that idea. The higher the strategic fit, the more appropriate it is to keep or share an idea than to sell it. In line with the Three Horizons model, which we've superimposed onto Figure 6 as a basis for comparison, your priority should be to improve your capability first in areas that are strategically aligned to your core businesses, because this is where you are likely to generate the highest returns.

At the same time, you should be making exploratory investments, in order to give yourself broad technological options for the long term. As these un-aligned innovations develop, and as the markets they represent mature, your investments should move left and up the grid, until eventually they become core businesses themselves. Some will have been abandoned or divested along the way, but those that make it should leverage your unique strengths to generate equally high returns.

A balanced portfolio, such as the fictitious one in Figure 6, should also enable you to flatten out the peaks and troughs in your innovation efforts.

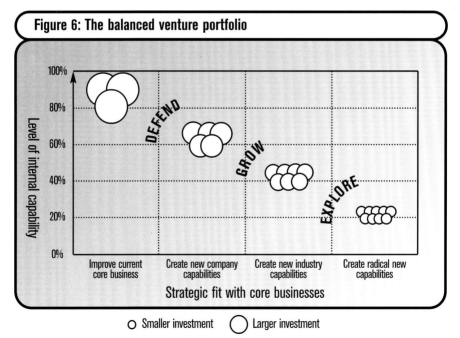

Figure 6: The balanced venture portfolio

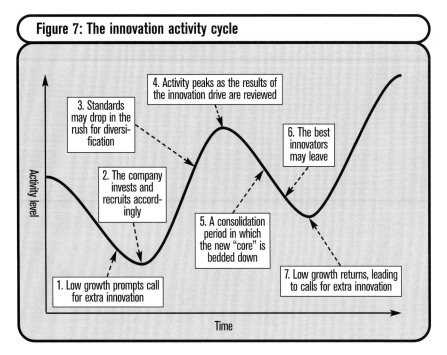

Figure 7: The innovation activity cycle

3. Standards may drop in the rush for diversification

4. Activity peaks as the results of the innovation drive are reviewed

6. The best innovators may leave

2. The company invests and recruits accordingly

5. A consolidation period in which the new "core" is bedded down

1. Low growth prompts call for extra innovation

7. Low growth returns, leading to calls for extra innovation

Activity level

Time

As we'll discuss further in Chapter 3.4, DSM, the Dutch producer of nutritional and pharmaceutical ingredients, specialty materials and industrial chemicals, has traditionally seen its level of innovative activity cycle every 10 years. Similar cycles have been observed in a number of leading organisations by Rob Kirschbaum, vice-president of innovation at DSM, and by other members of the H-I Network.

The typical stages of the cycle are illustrated in Figure 7. The problem with such peaks and troughs is not necessarily the frequency but the amplitude. If with each cycle you lose your best people then you will find over time that your human resources become severely depleted. A cohesive, open innovation strategy may not be able to flatten out the peaks and troughs completely, but it should certainly reduce their amplitude.

New Business Traffic Lights

Even if you plot your investments on a venture portfolio grid, as demonstrated in Figure 6, you may still find it difficult to decide which to keep, share or sell. Accordingly, we recommend the use of a tool called "New Business Traffic Lights," developed by Andrew Campbell at Ashridge

Strategic Management Centre and published in the previous H-I Network report *Winning Ideas for Strategic Growth and Venturing*.[5] This tool was inspired by Tim Hammond, corporate development and group marketing director at Whitbread. It is intended to focus the minds of executives on the strategic case for each new business as much as on the financial case. Indeed, it reflects our view that the former can actually be more important than the latter.

The Traffic Lights are intended to concentrate resources on ventures that can clearly be shown a "green light" on four key criteria (see Figure 8) and at the same time demonstrate strategic alignment. They are designed to be used early in the life a project, before enough information is available to make a full financial business case, although they can also be used to review nascent business plans or ongoing ventures. Several leading organisations have introduced the Traffic Lights to end a dependence on net-present value calculations, forcing executives to consider factors such as value-advantage and the quality of leadership available for specific ventures. The four key Traffic Lights criteria are:

- **Value advantage over sharing.** Managers understand they need an advantage to succeed in a new sector, but they do not normally consider the

Figure 8: The New Business Traffic Lights

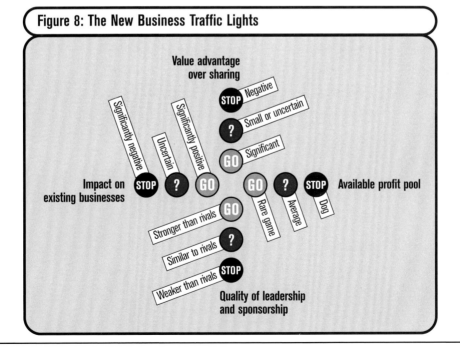

alternative of trading their advantage instead of using it to enter the new business. Capturing value from an innovation in the form of royalties rather than revenues could reduce risks and costs significantly in return for only a tiny fraction of potential returns. Disney, for example, routinely licenses its brand and characters to other companies.

● **Available profit pool.** Identify which innovations are likely to produce unusually low or high market returns, then ditch the former and concentrate on the latter. Under our definition, a "rare game" is one in which even a competitor with a disadvantage can earn a good return, while a "dog" is such a bad situation that it may prevent even an advantaged player from recovering their cost of capital.

● **Quality of leadership and sponsorship.** It's vital to have impassioned, high-quality leadership relative to rival businesses. As we'll discuss further in Chapter 2.3 of this book, it's equally vital for an innovation to be championed within the company.

● **Impact on existing businesses.** Managers take into account the benefits to or cannibalisation of existing businesses that can result from a new activity. However, they often underestimate the human resources that may shift away from the core as energetic managers are allocated to new business projects. New businesses can make claims on critical shared resources too.

The H-I Network researched and tested the Traffic Lights over a three-year period, during which time we found that any one green signal can be enough to clear a venture for further development, as long as there are no red signals. One red signal is enough to stop the venture, while a venture with all yellow signals is marginal.

It's important to point out that the Traffic Lights do not take execution issues into account, such as whether suitable partners can be found or whether technology will work. Also, they do not provide clear stop/go decisions for every situation. However, they frequently give a "stop" answer in situations where managers are inclined to "give it a try". As a result, they screen out a larger percentage of new business projects that would subsequently fail.

2.2 Process

There's no single correct way to structure an innovation process. Some elements will always be specific to particular organisations or industries. However, most leading innovators tend to subject ideas to the same basic stages of research, development and commercialisation. Figure 9 on page 42 illustrates just some of the various names given to these stages by different organisations and individuals that we have encountered during our research and advisory work.

At the top of this table are the generic names we prefer to use. You'll notice we are alone in using "Realise Value and Learn". Few organisations at present regard this as a discrete stage. That is to say, most don't have a mechanism in place for embedding all they have learned about a particular innovation while extracting value from it. Furthermore, most organisations still have processes in which the teams handling each stage simply "throw each idea over the next wall" once they are done with it. The communication between these teams tends to be linear and perfunctory. In the resulting environment, it is difficult to correct the course of an idea, or to abandon it, as circumstances change.

To refer back to Figure 3 on page 25: if the right-hand side of the bow-tie changes in the run-up to commercialisation then further activity on the left-hand side may be required. Your scientists, engineers, marketers and sales staff will not have their diverse needs aligned unless they talk frequently, an imperative we'll discuss in more detail in Chapter 2.3. Accordingly, the holistic innovation process we recommend requires ideas to be examined repeatedly from multiple angles, with continuous communication between the departments involved.

Most organisations fail to embed all they learn about an innovation after it is developed

In some respects, this process is linear. For example, we recommend you:

- establish a phased approach with clear milestones and accountability throughout;

Figure 9: Innovation processes in corporates

	Ideas pipeline	Concept	Feasibility	Design and develop	Implement and trial	Operate and improve	Realise value and learn
Major oil company	Opportunity domains	Ideas	Feasibility	Capability building	Launch	Operate and grow	
Major energy company		Appraise	Select	Design	Execute	Operate	
FMCG producer		Evaluation	Feasibility	Design and prototype	Implementation	Pilot	
Telecoms company		Concept	Proposition development	Accelerator	Commercial launch	Value realisation	
Commercial airline		Exploration	Feasibility	Development	Build and trial	Launch	
FMCG producer		Exploration	Development	Trial	Implementation	Consolidation, improvement and operation	
Aerospace engineering firm	Opportunity list	Opportunity Assess-1	Opportunity Assess-2				
Manufacturer		Ideas screening	Feasibility	Business case definition	Development and validation	Scale-up	
Consultancy	Intent and filter	Concept	Shape	Build	Scale		
Academic		Level 1 – Concept Generation	Level 2 – Business Evaluation	Level 3 – Proposition Development	Level 4 – Implementation		
Utilities provider	Workshop/intranet	One-pager	Five-pager	Proof of concept	Venture plan	Launch	

- establish clear "gateways" (stop/go assessments based on increasingly tough criteria) in the development of individual innovations, to limit financial exposure;

- be quick and ruthless about stop/go decisions, since shedding mediocre ideas accelerates the ones that will ultimately generate most value; and

- consider a "timetable" approach to new venture launches, under which projects compete for the next window in a cyclical schedule, to ensure you have the capacity for new roll-outs.

Of course, it takes more than glorified box-ticking to ensure your innovation process is both holistic and strategic. A cultural shift throughout your organisation may be required. The Five Ps will, as a whole, ensure you create the right environment for innovation. Within this environment, you will need to ensure your new processes are understood and embraced fully by all those with a stake in them. To this end, you should:

- invest sufficient time to align senior executives around the purpose, scope and ambition of your new processes;

- run co-ordinated communications and programme management to ensure a strategic fit with the wider business, and to support the culture change;

- encourage and coach individuals to show initiative in pursuing innovations – rewarding them with responsibility, creative freedom and resources – thereby improving and extending their skills, giving them a more external perspective (see "Extrapreneurs" on page 54), and transferring their skills across the organisation;

- build an organisational skill-set that enables the process to be sustainable; and

- involve operating units in both the innovation and commercialisation process, supplying individual ventures with individuals who are passionate about those ventures.

Ultimately, the innovation process must be allowed to develop iteratively and continuously. In an open innovation environment, there is no room for planning approaches that stick rigidly to specific time-horizons and thereby allow ventures to go ahead regardless of how circumstances change during research, development and commercialisation. The prevailing attitude must be one of entrepreneurialism and opportunism.

The New Business Cube

To help organisations think holistically at all times, we devised "The New Business Cube" in figure 10. It illustrates the nine key success factors that executives should consider repeatedly during the development of an idea, namely:

1 Customers and market opportunity. In which markets will this innovation meet clearly defined needs? And who will want to buy it once it is fully developed? As illustrated in Figure 3 on page 25, you need to consider the right-hand side of the bow-tie as early as possible in the innovation process. Considering this criterion is essential to ensure you invest on the basis of "market pull" rather than merely "technology push". And it must be considered repeatedly, in case conditions in the target markets change.

2 Product or service proposition. Will this innovation really have significant applied benefits once it is fully developed? Are you over-emphasising the importance of the technology involved and thus over-estimating its value? If in doubt, remember the old Apple slogan: "It's not how powerful the computer is, it's how powerful the computer makes you."

3 Competition and alternatives. Do rival products or services exist that could prevent you from winning a sufficient share of your target market, or that could nullify the prospects for your innovation altogether? In our experience, many companies invest significant amounts of time and money into innovations before performing even the simplest check – say, a Google search – to see whether their rivals are doing anything similar.

4 Strategic fit and business model. Should you be pursuing this idea as an organisation? Does it fit your business model? And if not, is it so significant that you should change your business model to accommodate it? This is the key criterion on which to assess whether an idea should be kept, shared or sold.

5 Management team and partners. Organisations typically divorce ideas from people. That is to say, they hit upon a great idea and pursue it without considering early enough who will actually implement it upon development. For example, you may have a great idea to extend part of your business into

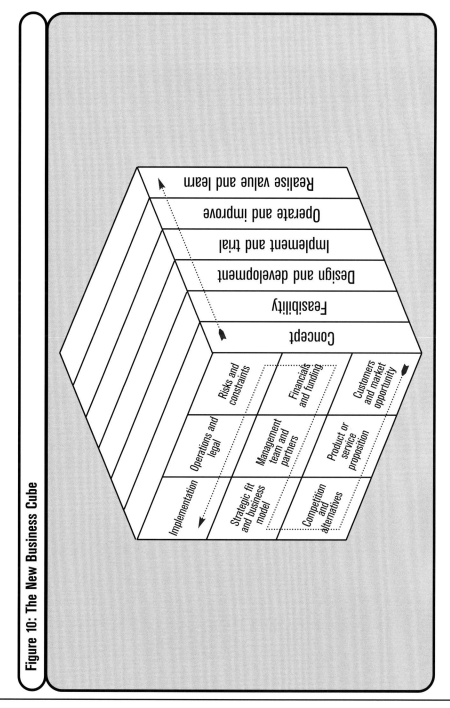

a new territory, but if you don't have the right people willing to go and work in that territory then you've got a serious problem. For each new innovation, you need to consider: who's going to champion and deliver the value at the end of this development process? Or, alternatively, whom should we partner with to extract value from this idea? Accordingly, the New Business Cube regards people as central to the innovation process.

6 Financials and funding. Is this idea going to produce a product or service with enough scale and significance to make it worth doing? And if so, how are you going to fund it? Have you got enough free resources, or will you need partners? Meeting this criterion is obviously essential to the progression of an idea through the "gateways" mentioned above.

7 Risks and constraints. Most companies try to weigh up the risks and constraints facing an innovation at the start of its development, but few do so continually throughout the innovation process. This is a recipe for disaster, notwithstanding the globalisation of both supply chains and markets. If you expect to serve a particular territory with a particular product and the local political situation deteriorates, where does that leave you? If you intend to launch a new service in a highly regulated market and the law changes, should you adapt or abandon that service? More fundamentally, should you risk the reputation of your group's brand – no matter how compelling the individual idea – by entering an industry where you have no experience?

Few companies weigh up the risks facing an idea throughout the innovation process

8 Operations and legal. Will your organisation have the right operating and legal structures to turn this innovation into a business?

9 Implementation. When considering any complex task, it's helpful to consider the next action required to complete it. This is the purpose of the final criterion on the New Business Cube: no matter which stage you are at, consider what remaining assessments of the idea you need to make, and what actions need to be performed in order to further its development.

As illustrated in Figure 10, each of these considerations needs to be made at each of the following six stages:

1 Concept

2 Feasibility

3 Design and development

4 Implement and trial

5 Operate and improve

6 Realise value and learn

The status of some of the assessment criteria may remain the same throughout the process, but most innovations, during the course of their development, will not stand up to scrutiny in all nine areas at all times. Indeed, a typical corporate mistake is to make an holistic assessment only while an idea is at the stage of, say, a two-page SWOT analysis. Such an oversight can lead not only to wastage, as innovations veer off in the wrong direction, but also missed opportunities.

The Business Cube can alert you to wasteful imbalances in your innovation process

As advisers we have witnessed such mishaps on several occasions, among leading companies. For example, a major utility company in the UK recently thought it had come up with a brilliant innovation only to discover, upon examining this innovation through the lens of the New Business Cube, that it lacked the necessary people (owing to redundancy), and that as an organisation it lacked the necessary skills. It also realised that the idea was not nearly as scaleable as it had originally thought, making its investment in the innovation to date wasteful.

In the past, companies have tended to set and deliver only the most stable, inflexible plans. The New Business Cube aims to embed an iterative process in your innovation strategy so that ideas can be modified on the fly while holistic planning takes place at every stage. It can alert organisations to imbalances in the development of particular elements of their new products or services. By keeping an eye on all nine criteria during the journey to commercialisation, you can minimise waste, adapting or abandoning each idea as necessary.

Ancillary innovation processes

Different organisations obviously have different priorities when it comes to overhauling their innovation processes. They may wish to tap a stockpile of dormant IP, for example, or to balance their venture portfolio by investing in innovations with a long-term development horizon. Professor Julian Birkinshaw of London Business School and Andrew Campbell of Ashridge Strategic Management Centre recently identified four types of innovation process that put the emphasis on very different sources of ideas and strategic outcomes. It's worth recapping these types, to explain where they remain instructive and where they have become inadequate:

● **Private equity venturing**

This term refers to the efforts of an organisation to invest in start-up businesses for the purpose of purely financial gains, as if it were an independent venture capital fund. Today, most companies that operate such a fund tend to use it for strategic purposes – they invest in start-ups chiefly to option technologies that could be of use in the future. A secondary benefit of the strategic approach is that by investing in really promising technologies you can hedge against the possibility that you will pick the wrong technological direction in which to take your organisation. You may also be able to prevent really promising technologies from disrupting your markets. A good example is the independent venture fund set up in 2006 by Tate & Lyle, the food and industrial ingredients manufacturer (see Chapter 3.5).

● **Harvest venturing**

This term refers to the conversion of existing resources into commercial ventures. Such resources may be surplus to the core business, as in the case of dormant IP, or marketable to external customers, as in the case of specialised consulting teams. A unit with a harvesting remit tends to be passed ideas that, in spite of their potential value, cannot be divested immediately. It will evaluate, invest in and develop those ideas to the point where they can attract interest from outside buyers.

Recently, harvest venturing has fallen out of fashion as organisations have realised that converting surplus ideas into cash may offer bottom-line gains in the short-term but create a serious drain on talent. Nevertheless, a harvesting initiative can be a useful way to energise the core innovation process. Recently we helped 100 scientists from a leading global company to carry out a New Business Cube analysis of all the innovations they working on, and thereby identified 12 ideas that merited a first- or second-level business plan. Some of these ideas had the potential to become spin-out companies. Others were able to be exploited immediately within the existing business. The bottom line is that a conscious harvest-venturing initiative may enable you to spot opportunities where you didn't see any previously. It is not an holistic approach to innovation in itself, but it can help you to identify "false negatives".

Harvesting is not an holistic approach to innovation, but it can be a valuable adjunct

● **Ecosystem venturing**

This refers to the use of venture capital funding by a large company to support suppliers, customers and even providers of complementary products and services. Its aim: to buy access to certain technologies or simply to foster relationships that make collaborative innovation more likely. Today, of course, open innovation makes such arrangements necessary regardless of whether a corporate venture fund is involved. The term can however be confusing given the proliferation of "green" technologies.

● **Innovation venturing**

This broad term refers to the use of traditional methods from the venture capital industry in innovation processes. An innovation venturing unit is one that operates alongside an R&D function to invest in promising ideas, put them on a fast-track to commercialisation and reward their creators proportionally. You may hear it applied to open innovation mechanisms such as accelerators, incubators or, in the case of Shell, "GameChangers" (see Chapter 3.3).

2.3 People

Even the most brilliant innovation can be squandered if it doesn't have the right people involved in its development. This may sound an obvious point, but it's one that many organisations fail to grasp fully. Most recognise it's important to pour talent into innovation project teams – after all, as any independent venture capitalist will tell you, it's better to back a good team with a mediocre idea than a mediocre team with a good idea. Nevertheless, many fail to ensure the right people are in place to provide the right support at the right time.

As we have discussed above, one of the main principles of open innovation is that knowledge from a variety of sources can and should be tapped during research, development and commercialisation. In terms of human resources, this means assigning different people to an innovation at different stages of its development. The skills and attitudes that serve a project team well in the early stages may become inappropriate or even counterproductive later on, as the exploration of possibilities gives way to the number-crunching reality of commercial operations. Indeed, our research shows that most project teams related to specific innovations have a high churn of staff beyond a small, hard core.

However, it is important not to fall into the trap of believing that the entrepreneurial impetus for an idea can always be "parachuted in". Larger companies have a tendency to divorce ideas from the people who came up with them. They expect a corporate-allocated team to have the passion and motivation to drive through these ideas. But our research and advisory experience has shown us this is rarely the case. Recently, we met a group of managers at a leading company who had come up with the idea of opening a branded chain of pizza restaurants. Their company had no experience in the food service industry, so we asked about the origin of the idea. It turned out the underlying innovation was a highly effective, cholesterol-lowering dough. The innovation process at this company was so focused on commercialising ideas that it had forgotten to involve the inventors, who were arguably in a better position to explore the

> **Many organisations fail to ensure they have the right staff for each innovation stage**

Figure 11: Essential roles in innovation processes and projects

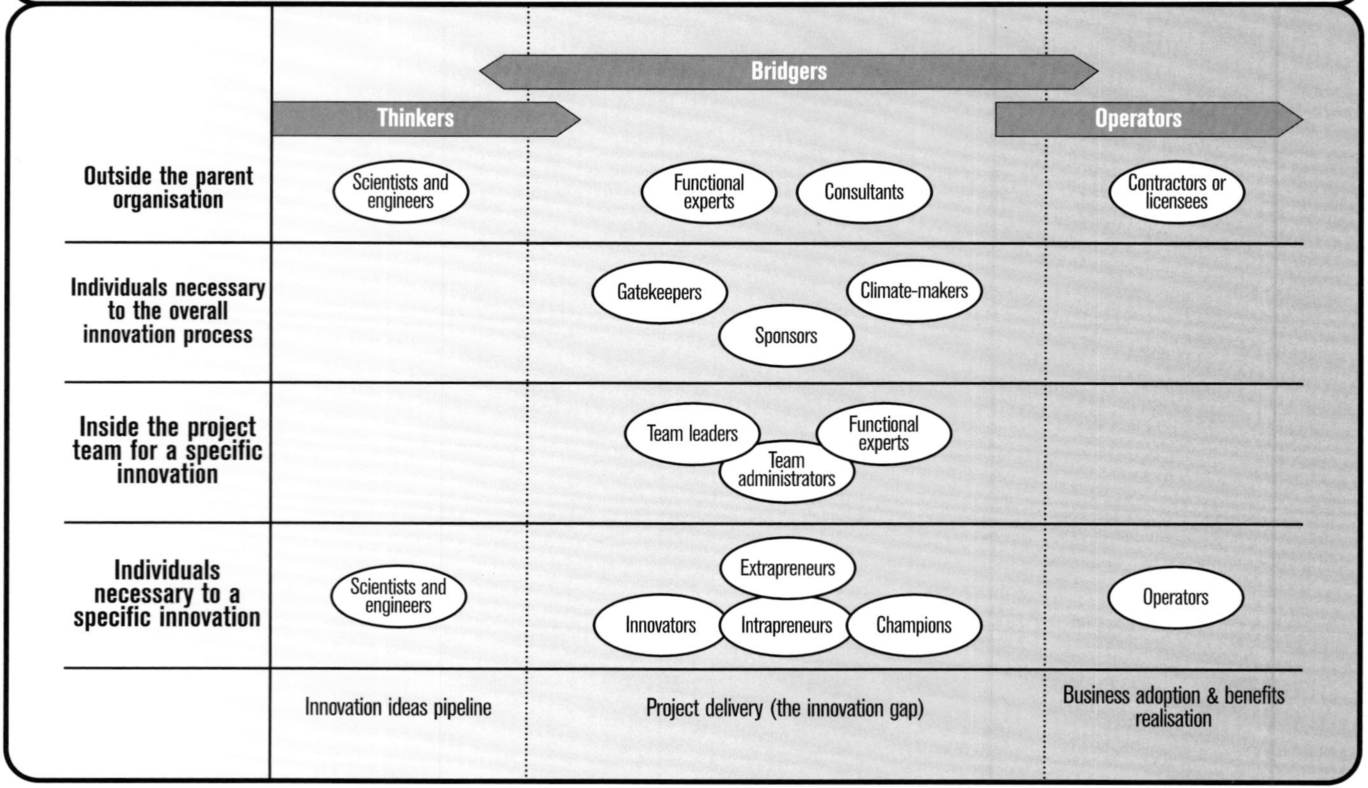

	Thinkers	Bridgers		Operators
Outside the parent organisation	Scientists and engineers	Functional experts · Consultants		Contractors or licensees
Individuals necessary to the overall innovation process		Gatekeepers · Sponsors · Climate-makers		
Inside the project team for a specific innovation		Team leaders · Team administrators · Functional experts		
Individuals necessary to a specific innovation	Scientists and engineers	Innovators · Extrapreneurs · Intrapreneurs · Champions		Operators
	Innovation ideas pipeline	Project delivery (the innovation gap)		Business adoption & benefits realisation

Source: *Innovation Leadership* (H-I Network, 2003), by Jill Hender.

capabilities of their new technologies and could therefore better-inform the commercialisation process.

As Figure 11 on page 52 illustrates, the typical journey of an innovation begins with "thinkers", idea-generators such as scientists and engineers; and ends with "operators", the people responsible for operating functions such as production, distribution and marketing. The sub-categories listed beneath sometimes overlap, with two or more applying to the same individual. They may even transform – for example, an innovator may become an intrapreneur, a project leader or even the CEO of a resulting spin-off. However, such instances are rare: thinkers seldom make good operators and vice versa. Hence, the success of most innovations depends on "bridgers", people who bridge the "innovation gap" between concept and commercialisation.

Most organisations know they need bridgers, but aren't clear about which types they lack. To determine whether you are in this situation, it will be helpful at this point to run through who does what during an optimally successful innovation development process.

The basic human ingredients

Under our definitions, thinkers generate ideas while innovators distinguish the applied benefits of ideas and determine a practical way to realise them. Meanwhile, the term "intrapreneur," coined by business consultant and entrepreneur Gifford Pinchot[6], is used to describe the person who is arguably the most important in the life of an innovation and certainly in its early stages. It is he or she who starts the process of implementing the commercial proposition, generates support and momentum for it in the organisation and, typically, ends up leading the project team.

Intrapreneurs share some of the characteristics of both independent entrepreneurs and traditional corporate managers. For example, they:

- are strong visionaries and "doers" with deep energy reserves;

- have strong technical and management knowledge; and

- tend to be motivated both intrinsically – i.e. by the pride and satisfaction of seeing a good idea to fruition – and extrinsically – i.e. through financial or other incentives.

An intrapreneur may also be the "champion" of an innovation – that is to say, they may be its chief advocate within the organisation, powering it through the various development stages with their belief and commitment. If they're not, then someone else must step in to this role. It has long been recognised that innovations need champions in large organisations if they are to be developed successfully, and there are many types of manager who may be suited to the role – line managers with technological expertise in the area of the innovation, for example, or more senior staff whose interest is piqued by the strategic potential of whatever idea is on offer. In effect, the champion is the first link in a chain of advocacy that should stretch to the top of the organisation (see "The process guardians," below).

Extrapreneurs

Maintaining an external perspective doesn't come naturally to large organisations, particularly where their innovation processes are concerned. That's why we coined the term "extrapreneur" ®, to describe the sort of individual who could overcome outdated habits and embrace open innovation principles.

Extrapreneurs have high levels of both external awareness and emotional intelligence. They have all the characteristics of an intrapreneur, plus a set of extra skills and capabilities, including: networking, influencing, negotiating and inspiration skills. Typically, they have experience in psychometrics. Certainly, they have good awareness of other people's personalities, motivations, attitudes, beliefs, behaviours, skills, likes and dislikes, strengths and weaknesses. They are also key players in determining the "exit" strategy for innovations – whether that exit takes the form of a spin-out company, a joint venture or an in-house launch among an organisation's existing products and services. They have a clear vision of where a venture should be headed in the medium- to long-term.

Innovations often face significant political barriers, particularly if they require a very different business model or organisational structure from that of their parent. We therefore see it as the job of the extrapreneur to provide political support and cover as innovations develop.

Consider Rick Wills, the former managing director of BA Enterprises, for example. In 1998, he was instructed by then-CEO Bob Ayling to form a unit to "build new businesses on the back of other assets." He had experience of this already – for example, he had helped to create a consulting business that would charge out BA managers to other airlines – so he knew that soft skills would be vital to the process of creating similar ventures. "The intrapreneur is battling against a lot of negative forces," he says.

Extrapreneurs have extra skills, an external perspective and exit opportunity awareness

Projects may be competing for resources or threatening the very existence of other units, he explains. Accordingly, they need to tap the organisation's knowledge without being treated as a competitor or a low-priority. "In BA Enterprises I didn't have tax experts or an HR expert or a corporate M&A expert, or an international law expert; I got those skills from within the mothership, from within the corporation of BA," he continues. "They had their day jobs to do and supporting me wasn't their priority, but establishing [a] network, using these influencing skills, meant that I could get all this expertise on board to help."

As far as external awareness is concerned, it is the duty of the extrapreneur to help overturn the traditionally inward-looking nature of the large organisation. Extrapreneurs keep an eye on markets, technologies, socioeconomic trends and best-practices. As Mr Wills puts it, they are experienced "landscapers", providing innovations with a market context. In this they are proactive: for example, BA's executive jet business was supported in its early stages of development by research on changing travel habits from the Henley Centre, which Mr Wills commissioned.

Extrapreneurs are also conduits through which external ideas can flow into the organisation. They facilitate the building of external partnerships, they manage the boundary between new ventures and the core business and they plagiarise industry best practice in all areas of the innovation process.

The project team

It's obviously vital to get the right balance of people in the project team for a specific innovation. Most organisations recognise they need adequate technological expertise and administrative capability here. However, many also neglect the development of team leaders. As a result, they may promote, say, innovators without the necessary leadership skills. In effect, they underestimate how important those skills can be at even the earliest stages in an innovation's development.

It is the responsibility of the leader to ensure their team has access to the differing skills, experience and attitudes required at each stage of the innovation process. And this is no small task given that people who are innovative, and who can thrive in the dynamic environment of a new venture, tend to be non-conformists. Our research shows that to avoid harmful clashes between staff, project leaders should recruit primarily on the basis of values, as well as functional expertise or specialist knowledge. They should also prize good track records over raw potential.

An important consideration for the oversight of an innovation process is that team leaders are not necessarily capable of transforming into the CEOs or MDs of resulting ventures or spin-offs. A different style of leadership is certain to be needed in the commercialisation phase, and that may require the hiring of a more experienced pair of hands.

The process guardians

Just as every innovation needs an internal champion, so it also needs an internal "sponsor", a high-level executive who provides advocacy, political support and, crucially, the resources an innovation needs to develop. In decades past, such an individual would have been found on an *ad hoc* basis, as a scientist or engineer fought to have their idea recognised and appreciated. Today, they're proactive in communicating with extrapreneurs – for example, through the Innovation Centre at DSM, the Dutch manufacturer of nutritional and pharmaceutical ingredients, specialty materials and industrial chemicals (see Chapter 3.4).

Sponsors may be senior line managers, members of the board or even non-executive directors, but whatever their origins they must have courage, determination and, crucially, time. Once attached to a specific innovation, they typically make it their business to carry out the following tasks:

● evaluation;

● monitoring;

● coaching and advising members of the project team; and

- protection from the "corporate immune system" in the form of, say, ringfenced funding.

They should also help to ensure knowledge acquired during the development of one innovation is made available to all other project teams – for example, through a leaders' forum.

We use the term "gatekeepers" in Figure 11 to describe an individual who directs information from outside the organisation to the relevant person inside – for example, they may forward unsolicited business ideas to staff who will receive and evaluate those ideas without prejudice, whether or not they pose a threat to the organisational core. The term "climate-maker" refers to a senior executive who does not intervene in specific projects as a sponsor but works to foster extrapreneurial freedom more generally throughout the organisation.

The importance of external talent

As discussed in Chapter 1.2, organisations are increasingly finding they can add value to innovations, and accelerate their development, by tapping external expertise. However, our research indicates that, in situations where external specialists make a positive impact on specific innovations, they are often being recruited too late. It is important to understand where a venture is going before bringing in such a person, and we would expect this process to take up to six months from the point that an innovation is given its first development approval. However, many organisations wait up to 18 months. As a result, they waste resources and value-creation opportunities.

External specialists can add value, but are typically recruited 6-18 months too late

One innovation that benefited recently from the arrival of an industry expert, and later became a highly successful venture, was Alleggra, the soy-based egg substitute. This Unilever spin-off was originally intended to be a food service business, supplying dry-mix products to large kitchens. However, when Stephen Manley, a successful entrepreneur, was brought in as non-executive chairman, he recognised the business could extract far more value from its innovation by marketing it as a food ingredient to manufacturers of, say, baked goods such as cakes and quiches. Mr Manley changed the market positioning of the business, and the profile of whom its customers should be. In effect, he defined its strategy from an external perspective rather than a corporate perspective.

Mr Manley has also been influential in determining the appropriate executive team to drive the business forward. Ultimately, Unilever leveraged his expertise and perspective, which they could not have developed internally, to ensure they assembled the right team and steered it in the right direction as quickly as possible.

Organisations that fail to assign external specialists to their new businesses run the risk of being misinformed by their incumbent staff. To keep a venture alive, those running it may act as if all is going well when the reverse is true, but an external venture capitalist or experienced non-executive director won't tolerate such behaviour. In the future, expect to see extrapreneurs marketing themselves in the same way that non-executive directors currently do, on the basis of specialties in particular industries or company development stages

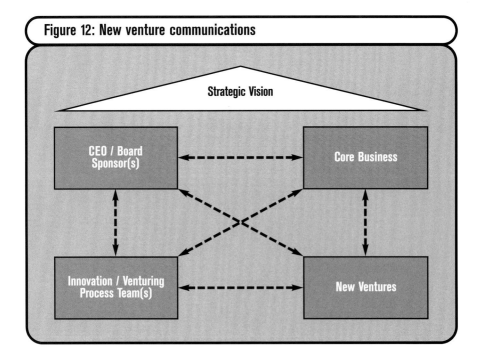

Figure 12: New venture communications

Strategic Vision

CEO / Board Sponsor(s)

Core Business

Innovation / Venturing Process Team(s)

New Ventures

Crucial communications

Figure 12 illustrates the need for two-way communication in all directions across the innovative organisation. It's particularly relevant to organisations that have a corporate venture unit, where new ventures may need their own "microclimate" – a structure and/or culture very different from that of their parent.

One of the key objectives of corporate venturing is to generate knowledge, capabilities and experience that could be of use to the core business, in line with the "Realise Value and Learn" phase described in Chapter 2.2.

Many organisations fail to appreciate that new ventures will divert talent from their core

Thus, knowledge has to flow from ventures back to both the venturing process teams and the core business. It is our belief that an extrapreneur is required to create and maintain these links effectively.

As discussed above, the overall vision must provide the strategic context for the innovation process. Meanwhile, we define the "process team" in Figure 12 as the collection of units and individuals whose joint responsibility is to ensure innovations are identified, researched, developed and commercialised optimally. The team manages the organisation's portfolio of innovations; helps assemble and monitor the management teams of new ventures; formulates exit strategies as necessary; and determines the formal reporting and remuneration structures unique to each venture. It is typically led by a senior executive who reports to whichever board member is chiefly responsible for strategy.

To some extent, the arrows in Figure 12 also represent potential flows of people. Many organisations fail to appreciate adequately that their new ventures will divert people from their core. New ventures have a high likelihood of failure but are always a good opportunity for organisational learning. Thus, processes need to be in place to absorb venture teams back into the core, and to embed the lessons they have learned, if things don't go according to plan.

2.4 Partners

Innovation is by definition a move into the unknown. If you're trying to turn a raw concept into something valuable then you'll need to harness new competences and capabilities, whether you generate these for yourself or buy them in from someone else. In a closed innovation environment, the former approach is king: organisations tend to "learn by doing", or to acquire knowledge via recruitment and company-acquisition. By contrast, open innovation thrives on partnerships, in which different organisations take responsibility for different stages of research, development and commercialisation, depending on what each partner does best.

Provided such deals are handled correctly, they can make an innovation process faster, cheaper and more effective. As discussed above, many companies now ask themselves as a matter of course whether they should share their new ideas – to do otherwise, they believe, would be just as reckless as ignoring opportunities for outsourcing or offshoring. Take Unilever, the fast-moving consumer goods company, for example. Every company in its venture fund portfolio must identify a potential partner for further investment or development within two years of being backed. Otherwise, Unilever has the following attitude: "If we can't find someone else to buy into this idea then why should we?"

If you want to innovate then you're sure to need new competences and capabilities

Moreover, in some situations, partnering is essential. You still cannot realistically do business in China, for example, without the help of other organisations in your industry, even if you have a wholly owned business in the country.

Then there are partnerships based on venture capital (VC). By partnering with an external VC fund, a company may be able to: leverage the sectoral expertise of the fund managers; gain valuable insights about deal-flow and technological trends; and find it easier to source external talent for specific ventures. Most importantly, it should be able to generate a financial return from the fund, using its own expertise where possible to boost the value of the portfolio companies. Aligning venture capital with corporate strategy can be: indirect, as in the case of the life sciences fund administrated by Burrill & Co. in San Francisco and supported by many leading companies including Unilever, DSM and Nestlé; or direct, as in the case of Intel Capital, which has invested in around 1,000 companies since 1991, often as the lead investor. The challenge in both instances is to ensure your investments are managed just as they would be in the external VC industry, with equivalent roles, expectations, strategies, metrics and remuneration packages. Otherwise, you may find it difficult to find external partners for internally generated ventures.

Making strategic alliances work

The term "strategic alliance" is used here to describe an arrangement that goes beyond the merely transactional. If you outsource a research task to an external specialist then you are practising open innovation, but your relationship with that specialist may be short-term. If, on the other hand, you contract a specialist to turn your intellectual property into a commercial proposition, a longer relationship – based on a licensing agreement or joint venture – may be required. The viability of an innovation may even depend on the continuous collaboration of several organisations throughout its lifecycle, as in the case of Senseo, the tabletop brewing system for gourmet coffee developed by Philips and Douwe Egberts (see page 23).

The benefits of a strategic alliance can be huge for organisations that successfully marry their complementary strengths. Great ideas can be scaled up and distributed globally; new markets and channels can be opened up; and technologies can be integrated to create a platform for numerous revenue streams. However, for a strategic alliance to be successful, each of the parties involved needs to be clear about how it will generate value from the deal, and that can be very difficult to predict during a venture's early stages.

Furthermore, a strategic alliance may require rival organisations to collaborate as never before. In such a situation, strength is required in both interpersonal relationships and Chinese Walls. For example, when Microsoft bought a 7% stake in Apple Computer in 1997, a line was drawn under decades of bitter rivalry between CEOs Bill Gates and Steve Jobs. The deal gave Microsoft some influence over its sexier rival. It also got an agreement that all new Apple computers would be preinstalled with Microsoft's Internet Explorer browser as standard. Apple, on the other hand, benefited from a $150m cash injection and a commitment from Microsoft that it would continue to develop software for the Apple Macintosh operating system. It also got a major boost to its market credibility.

Whether or not a partnership is controversial, it must be managed closely and structured flexibly. Perhaps the highest priority in the planning stages is to make sure that the interests of each party are considered holistically – the deal shouldn't be put in the hands of procurement people, for example, simply because its primary benefit is to cut costs. Any bias in the alliance may prevent its strategic vision from being aligned successfully with that of the parties involved. It will also render the deal less flexible, and therefore less capable of adapting to changed circumstances in the medium- to long-term.

When Tate & Lyle formed a strategic alliance with McNeil Nutritionals to produce Splenda®, the calorie-free sweetener, it initially shared responsibility for production and marketing. However, when the product took off, the deal structure could no longer provide adequate production capacity, and the relationship had to change. Tate & Lyle became the sole manufacturer, responsible for global sales to food and beverage manufacturers, while McNeil retained ownership of the Splenda® brand, with commercial responsibility for its retail and food service businesses (see Chapter 3.5).

A biased alliance will be difficult to align strategically and difficult to adapt

In our experience, a strategic alliance is more likely to succeed if it has one clear leader, in much the same way that an innovation is more likely to succeed if it has one clear champion within the organisation. A joint venture should be a discrete entity with its own governance and shareholder structure, to ensure it can operate in its own best interests without duress from either of its parents. This wasn't the case in 1998 when BT and AT&T, the telecoms giants, created a $10bn corporate solutions provider called Concert. The venture was wound up in 2002 by which time it was losing around $800m a year. Why? Partly because of tumbling call prices and overcapacity in the market, but also because neither of the organisations was willing to cede its relationships with big customers to the venture. In other words, neither was totally committed to the partnership.

Before entering a strategic alliance, it's vital for the prospective partners to consider every possible way in which the relationship might develop, and under what circumstances it would be appropriate for a partner to exit. What if you've overestimated market demand? What if the industry you intend to enter experiences a fundamental change? Scenarios should be thrown at the business plan to see what effects can be predicted, and flexibility should be given a high priority. In our experience, this approach is far more effective than simply reaching common agreement on a strategic vision for the alliance.

In terms of screening potential partners, due diligence should obviously be the order of the day. And every partner should be clear about every other partner's motivations for collaborating in the venture. As in any merger situation, cultural compatibility should not be underestimated, and all parties should be willing to share knowledge at an organisational level.

2.5 Performance

The old adage remains true: you can't manage what you can't measure. But how can you reliably set targets for innovation when it is by definition a journey into the unknown? Often the discovery of a great idea seems to result from serendipity rather than deliberate inventiveness. Accordingly, most organisations make little effort to calibrate their innovation process, despite the fact it is becoming increasingly vital to their competitiveness. Few go beyond revenue criteria in their analysis of individual ideas, and even fewer have metrics designed to monitor the performance of radical ones.

Setting targets for "internal rate of return", "return on investment" or "weighted-average cost of capital" is all well and good, but such values only really become meaningful when an innovation reaches its commercialisation phase – that is, when it becomes a proper venture. Similarly, a "net present value" calculation will not tell you whether an innovation is likely to succeed or fail. A product that performs poorly against short-term financial criteria may still go on to become highly profitable as circumstances change in its market, technology space or parent organisation.

As discussed above, a vital yet often overlooked determinant of whether you should proceed with an innovation in its early stages of development is "strategic fit". The value of an innovation that can be reasonably predicted in the short-term is, ultimately, less important than its contribution to the organisation's overall strategy in the long-term. This principle is especially important in industries such as oil and gas, where innovations may take a very long time to generate returns. You can learn more about how Shell manages its long-term innovation priorities in Chapter 3.3.

It's vital to judge individual ideas continually on their strategic fit

Companies driven by quarterly results can be tempted to abort long-term plans because these plans won't deliver benefits quickly enough. However, to sustain long-term growth through innovation, it's vital to judge individual ideas continually on their strategic fit. Pursuing too many digressive projects not only wastes resources that could be more fruitfully applied elsewhere but also makes it far more difficult to monitor the performance of the innovation process as a whole. As discussed above, it's best to build a portfolio in which projects can have their performance measured, and be benchmarked, using the sorts of tools that independent venture capitalists use to evaluate, prioritise or reject investments.

Of course, different types of organisation will have different priorities. For example, companies in mature industries or start-ups with limited capital may focus on total development costs. By contrast, companies in high-tech industries are more likely to evaluate new products on criteria such as product performance and time to market. In our *Innovation Performance Measurement* report, published in 2004, we determined that measures should not only assess the degree to which outputs achieve objectives (effectiveness metrics) but also the extent to which resources are utilised along the way (efficiency metrics). We also determined that in order for innovation performance measurement to encompass day-to-day operations, long-term strategy and everything in between, it needed to include both quantitative-objective and qualitative-subjective analysis.

Blending quantitative and qualitative analysis

Quantitative-objective analysis tends to be more appropriate in the latter stages of an idea's development – that is, towards the right-hand side of the open innovation bow-tie (see page 25) – when outputs become easier to define and predict. It tends to focus on technical processes, financial aspects and numerical outputs, with the key performance indicators and cost/return ratios of each new venture given tight definitions and monitored rigorously.

Qualitative-subjective analysis, by contrast, tends to be more appropriate in the early stages of development, where there is inherently more uncertainty. It is based on intuitive judgements and focuses on the performance of individuals, teams, groups or departments. The mechanisms it uses can include self-evaluations, supervisory ratings, peer ratings and external audits. Such things can in themselves improve information flows, networking, learning and shared understanding. However, planning and implementing an integrated regime of qualitative-subjective analysis is time-consuming, and requires management training.

Both quantitative and qualitative analysis can in fact be helpful throughout the innovation process. R&D has certain outputs – such as the number of patents filed or the numbers of new products released in a given period –

that may be subjected usefully to quantitative analysis, and be given targets accordingly. Equally, you may wish to set targets for how many ideas your organisation spins-in or develops in collaboration with

Have your customers' needs changed since the start of your idea's R&D process?

external companies, as Procter & Gamble has done with its aspiration to source 50% of innovations from outside the company.

Moreover, when an idea develops into a fully fledged venture, your qualitative-subjective analysis of it should not cease. Any business leader should continually ask themselves the question "Am I actually delivering what the customer wants?" but it's particularly important to do so at the start of a new corporate venture. At this time it's easy to be weighed down by baggage from your core business, and therefore miss the fact that your customers' needs have changed since the start of the R&D process. For example, it's no good measuring how often you deliver a parcel by 9am in the morning if your customer is thinking: "I don't care if the parcel arrives by midday so long as I know it's coming."

The politics of performance

To develop an innovation successfully, you may need to install it in a business structure very different from your that of your core, and with very different performance criteria. This can obviously be a source of friction if your core units and ventures are competing for resources on an internal market and/or occupy the same premises. And it can be explosive if the new venture uses different performance-related incentives. Communicating the role played by both types of unit in the fulfilment of the overall vision of the organisation is therefore crucial.

It may be necessary to give more independence to either individual ventures or the venturing process as a whole. For example, Tate & Lyle is giving its new Ventures fund as much independence as possible, according to CEO Iain Ferguson. "I think smart money finds smart ideas, and I think smart entrepreneurs find smart money; the kind of person who could screw it up is me," he says. The fund will be evaluated primarily on its financial performance. But its implicit role will be to improve the innovation potential of the core business. It makes sense for the managers of the fund, no matter how

Entrepreneurial change across the organisation is aided by consulting stakeholders frequently

independent they are, to leverage Tate & Lyle's expertise when making investment decisions and when advising their portfolio companies. Thus, Tate & Lyle should be alerted to emergent technologies, and have an "options box" of technologies to draw upon no matter which direction its markets take. You can find out more about the company's innovation strategy in Chapter 3.5.

From our research and advisory experience we have found that such communication is aided if senior managers – especially those in command of innovation processes – review the opinions of stakeholders on a regular basis. It may be helpful to interview, say, the R&D team about how they regard the venture team, and vice versa. Surveys of this type provide a measure for broad entrepreneurial change across the organisation.

A framework for holistic performance measurement

How can you balance the short- and long-term goals of your innovation process, while simultaneously analysing it on a quantitative and qualitative basis? The answer to this question differs between industries, but we believe that in all cases it involves five sets of considerations:

1 **Climate assessment.** Assessing your competitive environment is essential to the formulation of an effective strategic vision, and in turn your choice of innovation approach. It can be done relatively infrequently, but it must encompass prevailing business cultures and best practices in innovation processes, as well as in market conditions and general management.

2 **Strategic filtering of ideas.** If you have a central idea-filtering process then its performance should be measured. Analysis in this area could determine, say, how many raw ideas your organisation needs to reject before it comes up with something commercially viable. It could also determine: where the most suitable ideas are coming from; what can be done to encourage more; and how new ideas should be tracked alongside those already existing in the organisation for possible recombination.

3 **Innovation project management.** Your organisation may be good at managing capital projects, which are typically linear, but that doesn't necessarily mean it'll be good at managing innovation projects, which are typically iterative and dependent for their success on continual adaptation. Measuring the performance of an innovation before it is commercialised requires repeated qualitative analysis. In the context of open innovation, it requires the originating organisation to check external sources for potential rivals, with a view to sharing or spinning-in better technologies as necessary.

4 **Team effectiveness.** As discussed in Chapter 2.3, people are arguably the most important factor in the success or failure of an innovation, yet their performance as a team is rarely measured adequately. Psychometric testing and other methods of measuring "emotional intelligence" are therefore becoming more prevalent in the selection and monitoring of innovation project teams. Internal benchmarking, exposure to external investment and the recruitment of external specialists such as non-executive directors may also help.

5 **Portfolio measurement and valuation.** To make the right choices about which ideas to keep, share and sell, you need to find common or comparable measurement criteria for all the projects in your portfolio. These could indicate how risk is factored into emerging innovations or provide proxies for difficult-to-measure indicators such as return on investment. Whichever you choose, they must be visible and credible to all your stakeholders.

Additional questions you may wish to ask of your innovation process, to determine whether it is catering adequately for the long term, include:

- How many measures do you have that focus explicitly on innovation (as opposed to optimisation)?

- How many individuals in your company could say as much about your innovation performance as they could about your cost efficiency?

- How many people in your company have any personal performance metrics related to innovation?

- Do you systematically benchmark other companies on innovation (e.g. quantitatively in terms of, say, patents filed per year, or qualitatively in terms of, say, process benchmarking via networks or business academia)?

At most organisations, the innovation process is still driven by hard facts and short-term goals. We have found the companies that achieve the greatest success rely less on financial measures and have an approach that is communicated much more explicitly from the most senior to the most junior members of staff.

Significantly, very few organisations get external help to monitor their innovation performance systematically. This suggests that innovation performance measurement may stand today where financial performance measurement stood some 20 years ago. Given that open innovation is encouraging companies to look to external sources of knowledge for other reasons, the effect of external performance measurement on competitiveness could become significant in the near future.

2.6 Conclusion

The Five Ps are the foundations of an holistic innovation strategy. Once they have been considered and acted upon, the ongoing responsibility of the organisation is to embed the learning they represent, to ensure that as staff move away from the innovation process, or out of the organisation altogether, the framework for sustained and successful innovation remains in place. At the same time, the organisation needs to remain flexible: the process must not be so dependent on target-setting that it stifles entrepreneurialism.

There is no single right way of setting up an innovation process – the details will depend on the individual circumstances of a particular organisation, operating environment, industry or market. Nevertheless, the Five Ps should be a comprehensive aid to innovators at any organisation. They should ensure that good ideas are quickly identified and properly handled so that their value can be realised as quickly as possible.

What you learn from the Five Ps must be embedded in the organisation

Figure 13 overleaf illustrates which elements should be considered at which stages on the timeline of a typical innovation process. As we discussed in Chapter 2.2, different organisations may have different names for these stages, and for the individuals they involve, but we believe all are necessary elements in the development of any innovation. As such, they should provide a means to benchmark your process against that of your competitors. In concert with tools such as the New Business Cube, illustrated on page 45, and with the open innovation bow-tie illustrated on page 25, they should also enable you to marry your short-term steps to your long-term strategies without missing any opportunities to create value.

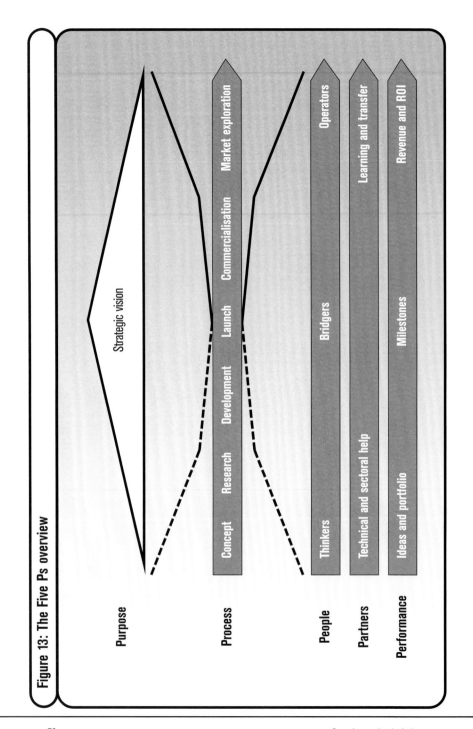

Part 3: Case studies

The following case studies demonstrate how open innovation is being put into action at five of the world's leading companies. As you will see, none of these companies is employing every element of the open innovation ethos as described in this book. Nevertheless, each has given its innovation processes much greater strategic alignment as a result of open innovation initiatives. Each has also recognised that generating an holistic innovation strategy is an iterative process requiring the organisation to embed all it has learned at every stage in the development of every idea.

The case studies are the product of in-depth interviews with senior executives responsible for innovation at:

- **Procter & Gamble (P&G),** which has set itself the target of sourcing 50% of its innovations from outside the company;

- **QinetiQ,** where end-market research is helping to add value to early-stage research propositions;

- **Shell,** where the "GameChanger" initiative is identifying radical new technologies with very long-term potential;

- **DSM,** where open industrial parks and the identification of emerging business areas are helping to concentrate innovation resources for maximum effect;

- **Tate & Lyle,** where the shift from commodities to added-value products and services is being driven by open innovation principles.

3.1 Procter & Gamble

Summary

- P&G has set itself a target of sourcing 50% of its innovation from outside the company, with the support of a pervasive leadership culture and incentives for accelerated research and development.

- Its open innovation framework, called "Connect + Develop", puts the emphasis on market needs, which are regularly assessed and prioritised.

- A mixture of proprietary and open networks helps to communicate P&G's specific scientific and engineering problems to huge numbers of potential collaborators.

- "Nested options" with external companies enable P&G to trial ideas that are potentially disruptive in single territories, without risking the investment necessary for a global roll-out.

Shortly after Alan G. Lafley became CEO of Procter & Gamble in 2000, he challenged the company to source 50% of its innovation from external sources. His definition of innovation was broad – it encompassed not only technologies and products but also advances in everything from business modelling to packaging. His aim wasn't to replace P&G's 7,500 researchers and support staff, but to leverage them better, applying their expertise to the search for problem-solving innovations outside the company as well as to the development of promising ideas within.

At the time, P&G was having its top-line growth outstripped by the costs of identifying, researching and developing good ideas – like so many other large companies. In spite of its huge resources, it could no longer monopolise the best knowledge in the fast-moving consumer goods (FMCG) sector. The company estimated that for every one of its researchers there were 200 scientists or engineers elsewhere who were just as good.

Thanks to Mr Lafley's vision, P&G chose to regard this situation as an opportunity rather than a threat. Its researchers knew from experience that when different business units combine their ideas, valuable innovations are

P&G now focuses on each idea's market readiness, rather than its point of origin

more likely to be discovered. So, Lafley, reasoned, with levels of R&D talent and expertise rising everywhere, it now made just as much sense to look for combinations of ideas between different organisations. In Mr Lafley's ideal scenario, half of P&G's innovation would come from its own labs, and half would go through them. By March this year, around 35% of the company's products included some kind of external element, up from less than 10% in 2000.

"It took us a few years to ramp up," says Nigel Trotman, associate director of External Business Development. "The initial focus was mainly in North America, but now we are truly global." He adds that Connect + Develop has galvanised the whole company thanks to a culture of pervasive leadership. Open innovation is "a truly corporate effort for P&G, driven from the very top of the company… We have been very public internally and externally about the top-down nature of what we're trying to do," he says.

P&G External Business Development is a cross-functional department whose members are situated throughout the company, Mr Trotman explains. "For each business unit such as 'Fabric Enhancers and Additives' we have a manager who defines external business development and open innovation strategy for that unit." He adds: "We think it's important to have innovation management systems in place that enable us, at each point of an R&D review, to have a discussion about whether the innovation in question stays inside the company or not, but we're not completely systematised. We tend to rely more on personal initiative among individuals and teams."

The "Connect + Develop" initiative

The key criterion on which P&G assesses ideas remains the same as ever: global scalability. "We are looking for solutions that improve the lives of the world's consumers," Mr Trotman says. However, it no longer expects to find such ideas solely among its own scientists and engineers. The company now practises open innovation under a set of operating principles and processes dubbed "Connect + Develop". Its focus now is not on where an idea originates, but on whether that idea has been developed to the point of prototyping, production or consumer interest. The faster it can be brought

Open Innovation in Action

to market, the better. P&G staff are incentivised to commercialise ideas quickly, and are thereby encouraged to seek external help.

Another consequence of Connect + Develop is that the search for innovations is driven not by "technology push" but "market pull" (see "The open innovation bow-tie" on page 25). P&G monitors the most widely expressed needs in its markets using the following tools:

- **Top ten consumer needs lists.** The company creates lists for each business and for the company overall. The latter includes broad, perennial ambitions such as "reduce wrinkles, improve skin texture and tone," and "create softer paper products with lower lint and higher wet strength".

- **Adjacencies lists.** These include new products or concepts that help P&G to take advantage of existing brand equity. For example, in oral care, it has expanded the Crest brand beyond toothpaste to include whitening strips, mouthwash and flosses.

- **Technology "game boards".** P&G tries to predict how technology acquisition moves in one area might affect products in other categories. This helps answer questions such as: "Which of our key technologies do we want to strengthen?" and "Among the technologies we already own, which do we want to license, sell or co-develop further?"

The broad areas of interest identified by these tools are communicated to a series of networks that P&G maintains independently or in collaboration with other organisations. Its proprietary networks include:

- **Technology entrepreneurs.** P&G has about 70 individuals working out of six "Connect + Develop hubs" in China, India, Western Europe, Latin America and the US. These are senior executives responsible for using the tools described above and translating the results into "technology briefs" that define specific problems. The technology entrepreneur's role involves everything from networking and patent research to scouring the shelves of local shops.

- **Suppliers.** P&G has a secure IT platform that enables it distribute technology briefs to its suppliers and gather proposed solutions confidentially. It exchanges staff with suppliers in so-called "co-creation" arrangements, which it says go "well beyond typical joint development," and ensures its senior leaders meet theirs on a regular basis.

P&G also works with several external partners to help it Connect + Develop. The following networks, some of which were started with P&G assistance, are all considered valuable to the Connect + Develop effort:

- **InnoCentive** is a company that maintains a Web-based network of around 75,000 contract scientists and that brokers solutions to tightly defined scientific problems.

- **Yet2.com.** Backed by a group of Fortune 100 countries including P&G, this is an on-line marketplace for intellectual property (IP). It works with clients to define what they're seeking or what they're making available for license or purchase, then brokers the resulting contracts to a global network of institutions including companies, universities and government laboratories.

- **The H-I Network** is a business alliance committed to fostering innovation and growth. Its membership comprises senior executives and key influencers at leading global organisations. The Network addresses business innovation process issues and thought leadership, and brings organisations together for "Joint Opportunity Assemblies".

Partnering with P&G

"If you want to share the risks associated with commercialising IP then you have to be willing to share the rewards," Mr Trotman says. For example, if a product will only be competitive when certain economies of scale in manufacturing and distribution are achieved, its creator may need the help of a partner such as P&G. To get that help, they may be asked to give up the rights to distribution channels or product categories in certain territories. "It's a resources game," Mr Trotman continues. Whether the IP in question is flowing into or out of P&G, "you just figure out who's best to handle it at each stage. If everyone is prepared to give up a little control, you can create real value."

He continues: "We have collaborated with many potential competitors, from small and medium-sized companies operating in our space through to companies who are operating in complementary spaces where there's a value-extraction opportunity in a non-competing business." He explains that Japan is an especially good source of open innovation because it has a highly fragmented FMCG sector and therefore many "excellent companies in our space who are not global". One product to be commercialised globally by P&G after emerging in Japan is the Magic Eraser, a stain remover based on a material called "melamine foam". It was spotted at a market by one of P&G's technology entrepreneurs. Now, thanks to a licensing agreement between P&G and the Japanese manufacturer, the product is being marketed across the US and Europe under the Mr Clean brand.

Sometimes, P&G will develop an innovation internally to the point where it looks extremely promising – e.g. on the basis of performance, initial consumer-qualification and preliminary marketing concepts – but where there are still "significant barriers to taking it to a national market straight away." In this situation, the company may decide to pilot the product in question by offering an exclusive licence to an external company in a particular territory. Under this "nested option", the external partner "would always have the rights to that channel, but if the product achieves certain milestones then P&G would have the rights to take back their learning" and scale it up to serve global markets. This learning might include consumer feedback, supply-chain issues or even something as simple as advertising copy. Alternatively, P&G may decide to divest the IP completely after the pilot has been running for some time. Overall, Mr Trotman says, this strategy is a good way to de-risk technologies that have the potential to be disruptive – if they fail to meet expectations then the remaining rights can be divested; if not, they may well end up generating billions of dollars worldwide.

Japan's fragmented FMCG sector is proving a great source of open innovation

Overall, Connect + Develop has ended the perception – both internally and externally – that P&G has to do everything itself. "P&G is open for business and collaboration," Mr Trotman says, adding: "We are the partner of choice." His organisation closed 100 deals with external companies last year, but that's not viewed as a major achievement. "Our footprint in Europe, in Asia, in many other markets is quite new," Mr Trotman concludes. "There are plenty of opportunities for us to find."

3.2 QinetiQ

Summary

● QinetiQ has become more effective at accelerating internal IP in recent years by focusing more on the potential markets into which that IP will eventually be launched.

● When approaching potential customers it no longer takes a "technology push" approach, pitching specific solutions. Instead, it seeks to open a dialogue about broad areas of difficulty the customer may be facing.

● The company is proving to be a rich source of IP for external companies. Its collegiate-style structure is helping to generating licensing, joint venture and spin-off opportunities.

QinetiQ is arguably the product of one of the world's biggest experiments in open innovation.

Prior to 2001, it was known as the Defence Evaluation and Research Agency (DERA), the exclusive research and development arm of the Ministry of Defence (MoD). DERA had formed gradually over decades as various high-tech and high-security sites were brought under one umbrella.

Around three-quarters of its staff ceased to be public servants to form QinetiQ, while the MoD remained their principal shareholder. The remainder formed DSTL (Defence Science and Technology Laboratory), which continues to do government work exclusively. QinetiQ entered a public-private partnership (PPP) arrangement in 2003, with the aim of commercialising its untapped resources – including around 5,000 unused patents – in the private sector. It was listed on the London Stock Exchange in February 2006.

The company now has 11,400 staff at more than 50 sites across the country, and some of the best research and development facilities in the world. It specialises in defence technology, but operates as an engineering contractor, licensor and service-provider in industries as diverse as healthcare and energy. It practises open innovation chiefly in two ways: (i) developing its own IP into licensing opportunities and spin-off companies, with the help of outside knowledge or facilities as necessary; and (ii) developing the IP of other companies by utilising its own competences and capabilities.

"The organisation has learned a lot over the past few years," says Stephen Lake, director of the company's New Business Accelerator team. He explains it used to depend too heavily on "technology push" – that is, on the promotion of specific commercialisation strategies for ideas originating within QinetiQ. "We were overselling our capabilities and getting into too much vapourware [software or hardware that is fails to emerge from its developer in spite of announcements to the contrary]." Now, he says, the company takes a much more open approach, based on identifying areas of mutual interest between itself and other parties.

In this, the New Business Accelerator acts as a kind of internal consultancy, shepherding good ideas from concept to commercialisation, and as a venture portfolio manager. Its various roles include:

- corralling good ideas, validating and developing them to ensure the organisation as a whole has a consistent flow of high-quality propositions;

- developing products from conceptual to market-ready status, "through the use of virtual and rapid prototyping";

- creating and delivering "go to market" plans;

- accelerating the development of businesses that perform well, helping to spin them out or install them in joint ventures if necessary; and

- providing advice, mentoring and interim management services throughout the lifecycle of each business.

Accelerating internal IP

QinetiQ has processes in place to capture any potentially useful idea from any member of the organisation. Indeed, everyone is encouraged to submit ideas, and to evaluate them based on so-called NABC criteria, standing for Needs (that is, customer needs), Approach, Benefits and Competition. "We have a pervasive entrepreneurial spirit, and we encourage idea champions," Mr Lake says.

One idea captured successfully by these processes was a runway debris detection system, now being marketed under the name of Tarsier. It was conceived by two of QinetiQ's radar experts, after the crash of Concorde flight AF4590 near Paris in 2003. The resulting commercialised system won an innovation award from the *Wall Street Journal* in 2005, and QinetiQ announced a £2m contract from Dubai International Airport in July 2006.

"This was an example of where we took most of the innovation and financial risk ourselves," Mr Lake says. "The business opportunity was in a sector close to our core business and our market validation showed the potential market size was significant. However, with such a disruptive solution it was absolutely key to find the right early-adopter customer. The early-adopter in this case was Vancouver, an airport that wants to be seen as leading in its use of technology to serve customers."

To get someone to be an early-adopter, "you need to paint them a picture of the future," Mr Lake says. He points out that QinetiQ now looks at innovations through "a broader market lens", considering from the earliest possible stage how each will be received by or even change the market in which it is eventually launched (see "The open innovation bow-tie" on page 25).

"To predict the ultimate size of a market, you have to consider the 'time to market adoption' of the product or service you're trying to commercialise," he suggests. "There's a whole bunch of stuff I put on ice because it was too early for its market – the best holographic computer-aided design system in the world, for example, in which we'd invested about $1m." If you're evaluating an innovation that you think could disrupt its market, you need to ask yourself: "Are there early-adopter customers to pull it through?"

Why good pitches address non-specific needs

"QinetiQ is proactive in looking for open innovation partners," Mr Lake says. He explains the company looks continually for "interesting spaces" where it thinks it can apply genuinely innovative thinking to major problems – whether in specific markets or, even better, cutting across several. It then creates solution "packages", perhaps involving virtual prototypes, to demonstrate how it can help potential customers in those markets.

"We contact organisations we think are early-adopter type customers," Mr Lake continues. "And what we ask them is this: 'We've been thinking about

Prospective partners can initiate contact with QinetiQ via one telephone number

10 minutes showing you something?' Some will say yes, some will say no, some will be cagey, some will say 'Actually, our biggest problem is x,' but the important thing is that most will respond. If, by contrast, we just called up and said: 'We've invented this widget, do you want to buy it?' then in most cases people would say no. It's a different kind of conversation."

Margins are also a crucial criterion on which QinetiQ judges the commercial potential of innovations. "If it's something manufactured, we look for a 50% gross margin," Mr Lake says. "If it's a business unit that doesn't fit so naturally with our existing capabilities then we would probably be looking for a 15-20% net margin. On the service side, it's different, because there are many different models in place, but in commercial services you're trying to get north of 10%. In traditional military support services, a margin of around 7% is pretty much dictated."

QinetiQ ensures prospective clients or collaborators can initiate contact too. It provides them with a single telephone number to call – marketed heavily during an early branding campaign called "Test Us" – from which they are directed to the right person within the organisation.

Mr Lake says one good example of a company extracting more value from its IP thanks to QinetiQ support is Intel. QinetiQ is working with the chip-manufacturer to develop "indium antimonide" processors, which offer huge speed advances without the corresponding heat that would be generated by traditional materials.

It has also recently developed a 3D foot-measurement system for Clarks, the UK shoe manufacturer and retailer. The aims of this digital last will be simple in the short term – to ensure customers buy footwear of the right size at Clarks' retail outlets and to demonstrate to them that the brand is investing in innovation. However, in the medium- to long-term it will gather data about geographical variations in foot size, to improve the company's inventory management, and it may ultimately enable Clarks to improve its designs.

3.3 Shell

Summary

- Shell's GameChanger programme aims to encourage innovators from inside and outside the company to suggest innovations with disruptive potential.

- The related vetting process helps to de-risk each idea to the point where massive R&D investment is justified, or where it may be appropriate to turn the idea into an internal business unit or spin-off company.

- Shell also sources innovations via technology scouts and themed workshops designed to forge partnerships with external companies.

- The long-term nature of oil industry projects makes it difficult to make accurate predictions about certain market needs. Accordingly, Shell invests heavily in scenario-building, based on distant horizons.

Could there be a disruptive technology lying dormant in the research and development (R&D) arm of your company? If so, how should you go about identifying it? And could you put it on a fast-track to commercialisation? In 1996, a senior executive at Shell realised that if he wished to find and exploit such a "game-changer", he would have to act more like a venture capitalist, investing in lots of small, high-risk projects.

Tim Warren was director of research and technical services in Exploration & Production (E&P), the largest of Shell's five divisions. In recent years, his team had come under increasing pressure to focus on the short-term needs of national operating units. As a consequence, it was spending very little time envisioning the types of technologies that could disrupt Shell's markets in future. The company was at risk of becoming a victim of technological disruption when, given its resources, it should be a beneficiary.

Shell was at risk of becoming a victim of disruption rather than a beneficiary

In an effort to get his staff dreaming up radical innovations, Mr Warren allowed them to devote 10% of their time to "non-linear" thinking, but the results of this initiative were disappointing. So, in November 1996, he went a step further and set up GameChanger, a small panel of business-savvy scientists and engineers whose brief was to stimulate "breakthrough" innovations, whether they originated at Shell or elsewhere, at selected universities and other partners.

GameChanger would identify ideas with disruptive potential and help their creators turn them into value-propositions, with the help of a $20m seed capital fund. It would then market the nascent ventures to relevant operating units, where they could be commercialised. Ideas without a significant technology component would continue to be pursued by a separate new business identification unit, while "evolutionary" ideas (non-gamechanging, low-risk) would continue to be pursued by dedicated teams within Shell's "Evolutionary Technology Development Programme".

By 1999, GameChanger accounted for four out of Shell's five largest growth initiatives

At first, GameChanger didn't generate many ideas, but it reached a tipping point after a three-day event designed to bring together Shell's most enthusiastic would-be entrepreneurs. The "Ideation Lab" was organised in collaboration with an external consultancy, Strategos. It was promoted to staff on the basis that any promising ideas it generated would win a share of $500,000 in development money. Seventy-two people attended, generating 240 ideas of which 12 were approved by the GameChanger for six- or 12-month funding. A few months later, GameChanger ran a five-day, follow-up event called "Action Lab", in which attendees were taught how to turn their ideas into business plans.

By 1999, the GameChanger process was beginning to make its mark. Ideas that originated in GameChanger now accounted for four out of Shell's five largest growth initiatives, and for 30% of E&P's R&D portfolio. By focusing on technologies with disruptive potential, it was increasingly influencing the direction of the company as a whole: for example, one of its ventures combined the efforts of units from across Shell to look at the many potential markets for renewable geothermal energy sources. The following year, GameChanger was rolled-out to all five of Shell's divisions, including corpo-

Open Innovation in Action

rate, where Group GameChanger was made responsible for innovations between and beyond existing businesses and was given a coordinating role.

The GameChanger process

Anyone can submit an idea to GameChanger via a two-page form on Shell's website. The people who do are generally Shell scientists and engineers, but any member of staff is welcome to contribute and, according to Leo Roodhart, the head of Group GameChanger, "10% of proposals are now from universities or external companies and individuals who wish to explore an idea for partnership with Shell."

Mr Roodhart adds that the company no longer relies solely on unsolicited ideas in its search for disruptive technologies: "We have 15 technology scouts within Shell who give up to 25% of their time to go to universities, conferences and trade shows," he says. Similarly, external companies are invited to regular "workshops" – each focused on a particular area of long-term opportunity – in which "the QinetiQs of this world [who have technology foresight]" help develop ideas that Shell may be best-placed to commercialise. "The only condition on all GameChanger projects is that they must have a Shell employee as a champion," Mr Roodhart says. "Who then develops the IP? That will be different in each case; but it does not always have to be Shell that owns it."

If an idea is deemed promising by its divisional GameChanger panel then the following process begins:

● The innovator is invited to provide further information in the form of a 10-minute pitch to the divisional GameChanger panel, followed by a 15-minute Q&A session. He or she can charge up to two days of their time to the divisional GameChanger budget while preparing for this presentation.

● If the idea is approved by the divisional GameChanger panel then it is forwarded to an extended panel – including "domain experts" – for a funding decision. In some cases, the GameChanger panel will raise questions that the innovators must address before the extended panel convenes. Innovators receive further funding during this test-and-mature phase.

● If an idea is approved by the extended panel then the innovator is given the authority and budget to assemble an informal project team. An "Action Lab" may be organised at this point to help the team scope the idea's potential, identify partnerships that could aid its commercialisation and plan the early stages of its development.

GameChanger's role is to consider broad disruptive influences in Shell's markets

● A few months later, the idea reaches a "tollgate" review, at which point its value-proposition must be defined in the form of a basic business plan. It may be abandoned at this stage owing to lack of progress, changed circumstances (in terms of, say, market conditions, regulations or technological obsolescence), or the loss of key members of the team.

There are generally two possible outcomes for any idea that clears all the hurdles above:

1 **Further R&D**. Even after proof-of-concept, an idea may need many years of research to turn it into a commercial venture. The GameChanger process effectively de-risks an idea to the point where such a long-term investment can be justified. Accordingly, most ideas that make it through the GameChanger screening process end up under the aegis of the Evolutionary Technology Development Program, with a dedicated execution team to turn them into ventures. After a period of incubation, an idea may transfer to an operating company where it becomes part of Shell's internal offering of goods and technical services. Alternatively, it may transfer to Shell's business accelerator to become a discrete business unit, a non-exclusive licensing opportunity, or an integrated solution for a Shell operating company.

2 **Conversion into a spin-off company.** A business unit called Shell Technology Ventures was set up in the 1990s to exploit research-ready patents lying dormant across the company, but the ideas it found were generally not sufficiently developed to form the basis for spin-offs. Since 2000, it has therefore worked increasingly with GameChanger. It has started over 20 companies, of which several originated in GameChanger, according to Mr Roodhart. To extract value from ideas aimed at other industries, Mr Roodhart recently set up a co-operative arrangement with a Scottish venture capital firm called ITI, which specialises in energy, medical and IT investments. Under this deal, ITI will help to find and vet investors interested in forming start-ups by licensing Shell technology.

Open Innovation in Action

The importance of scenario-building

Mr Roodhart says he agrees with the open innovation principle of channelling R&D resources based on market needs (see "The open innovation bow-tie" on page 25). However, he cautions, projects in the oil industry are so capital- and time-intensive that imagining how markets will look at their conclusion is very difficult. "McKinsey looked at the time between idea generation and 50% market penetration in various industries," he points out. "In FMCGs it was about one year; in pharmaceuticals, it was about seven or eight years; in communications it was about 10 years; in oil it was 20 years. Now, some people believe that in 20 years there may be no oil, so why the heck would we put money into it? This is why we spend so much money building scenarios."

He explains it is the Group GameChanger's role to think about the broadest possible disruptive influences in Shell's markets. "I have also set up an 'innovation coalition'," he says, "a loose network of all the people at Shell working on innovation and strategy including everyone whose job is to think about the long-term." This 60-strong team, described by Mr Roodhart as both a think-tank and a steering group, meets once or twice a year to discuss "future value spaces" for Shell such as bioenergy and clean coal. If the team feels Shell is lacking in one of these spaces, in terms of technology or know-how, it may recommend an open innovation approach to plug the gap.

Mr Roodhart suggests companies trying to search proactively for disruptive innovations need the following things:

- a vetting panel comprised of scientists and engineers with well-developed business sense;

- conditions and procedures that, ideally, enable innovators to break free from ongoing assignments to work on their ideas; and

- financial structures that allow promising ideas to be picked up by operational units as soon as they are ready for commercialisation, and not merely when the next budget round allows them to do so.

3.4 DSM

Summary

- DSM has put innovation at the heart of its culture, by encouraging staff to tap external resources; setting up open research facilities and venturing units; and setting up corporate venture capital to help develop a portfolio of emerging technologies.

- It believes different management styles are necessary at different stages of an idea's development – from scientists to intrapreneurs to professional managers.

- A series of strategic reviews recently helped the company to appraise its key strengths, determine which market needs it could most profitably serve in the future and identify key "emerging business areas" on which to focus its innovation resources.

The history of Dutch company DSM is one of continuous transformation through innovation. Established in 1902 as a coal-mining company (De Staats Mijnen, paraphrased in English as "Dutch State Mines"), it diversified throughout the 20th Century and now produces nutritional and pharmaceutical ingredients, specialty materials and industrial chemicals. It employs around 22,000 people at 270 sites worldwide and spends around €300m on research and development (R&D) each year. "As we understand it, innovation is a culture, not a process," says Robert Kirschbaum, the company's vice-president of innovation.

DSM has been shifting its focus to added-value products since the early 1970s, when the Netherlands closed down its state mines. Already a leading producer of fertiliser and other industrial chemicals, it began to focus on specialty chemicals, a process catalysed by its privatisation and public quotation in 1989. During the late 1990s, the company doubled its turnover to around €8bn through a combination of organic growth and acquisition, with the latter bringing considerable amounts of knowledge and expertise into the company. At the same time, it founded a new-business development unit, whose aim was to develop ideas – mainly from its own researchers – into commercial ventures that had a good fit with DSM's existing businesses.

During the early 2000s, it began to focus its resources on the key markets it serves today. For example, it divested its petrochemicals division in 2002; acquired the Vitamins & Fine Chemicals division of Roche, the Swiss pharmaceuticals giant, for €1.75bn in 2003; and acquired a materials business called NeoResins from the UK chemicals firm Avecia for €515m in 2005.

DSM regards partnerships as "a vital prerequisite for genuine innovation"

It also began to embrace open innovation. By 2000, it had committed around €25m to five venture capital funds focused on life sciences, biotechnology and performance materials, to secure options on a variety of emerging technologies. Then, in 2001, it set up a Venturing & Business Development unit with around 50 staff, whose brief was to use "both internal and external leads at all stages of… development," to accelerate the commercialisation of promising ideas. This unit would not be restricted to areas in which DSM had traditionally been strong. Rather, it would look for opportunities that DSM could "use, add or share", while leveraging its core competences to extract the maximum possible value. It has so far developed around 10 ideas into standalone businesses, both internal units and external spin-outs.

DSM has also invested in new sources of innovation. For example, in 2002 it set up an open industrial park, including an open R&D campus known as "Chemelot", in Geleen, the Netherlands. This park is home to many external chemical companies as well as DSM business units, with a common canteen that provides a hugely valuable cross-fertilisation of ideas, according to Mr Kirschbaum. DSM has also created a regional venture-capital fund in collaboration with local business angels and the regional government.

Chemelot represents part of a longstanding drive at DSM to apply more external knowledge to its innovation efforts. The company regards partnerships with external companies, universities and other organisations as "a vital prerequisite for genuine innovation," in that they allow it to be "re-inspired and refreshed with new ideas and new technologies." Mr Kirschbaum says another of the company's major priorities is to improve the business-sense of its scientists and engineers; as he puts it, to give them "a more intrapreneurial mindset".

Open attitudes to innovation

Mr Kirschbaum says different management styles are needed at different stages of an idea's development, from a scientific approach in the early stages to an "intrapreneurial" attitude at the point of commercialisation to a more risk-averse mindset once the business has matured. He contrasts scientists and intrapreneurs as follows:

Scientists...	Intrapreneurs...
• earn their reputations as individuals	• know that teamwork provides leverage
• get recognised for giving away knowledge	• get recognised for protecting knowledge (IP)
• tell people how to reproduce their work	• fear other people reproducing their work
• think economic feasibility doesn't matter	• consider economic feasibility paramount
• think the technology is everything	• recognise technology is only a starting point
• overvalue their contributions	• let scientists believe they are valuable

Mr Kirschbaum describes the conflicting views of intrapreneurs and managers, which must be resolved if a venture is to succeed, as follows. In this context, an "in-sultant" is a manager capable of "shaking the tree", preventing complacency in both specific ventures and the company as a whole.

Intrapreneurs...	Professional managers...
• feel consultants are needed	• feel "in-sultants" are needed
• are sales-oriented	• are profit-preoccupied
• create new revenue streams	• grow traditional revenue streams
• encourage rapid decision-making	• adhere to established policies and procedures
• stimulate a risk-taking attitude	• manage risk within boundaries

An innovation-led vision

DSM's strategic vision for 2010 stresses the importance of "market-driven growth and innovation". Mr Kirschbaum explains the company's innovation efforts must be part of a coherent strategy because it is not enough simply to identify promising technologies. "To create real value, you have to identify market needs, and then to identify which technologies can be adapted or developed to meet those needs," he says.

To identify the biggest market needs that it can serve in the future, DSM recently conducted a series of strategic reviews. These began with a consideration of the company's four chief knowledge clusters – that is, its chief sources of "technology push" – namely: performance materials, nutrition, industrial chemicals and pharmaceuticals. Eight senior executives were each given several months to consider how these clusters could generate the most value once certain trends had played out. They looked at societal trends such as the ageing Western population; rising health and safety awareness; and improved networking technologies. And at emerging technologies such as biotechnology and nanotechnology.

The team eventually identified four key "innovation pockets" that they felt represented the biggest commercial opportunities for DSM:

● healthy food and cosmetics, and pharmaceuticals;

● renewable, sufficient and clean resources;

● materials with advanced properties (e.g. lighter, stronger, more eco-friendly);

● electronics, information and knowledge systems

They then referred back to their assessment of DSM's existing strengths to determine where it should focus its innovation efforts. Ultimately, it identified four emerging business areas (EBAs):

● biomedical materials;

● specialty packaging;

● personalised nutrition; and

● "white biotechnology" (the use of living cells such as moulds, yeasts and bacteria, as well as enzymes, for industrial applications).

Mr Kirschbaum says this focus should help DSM to improve its portfolio approach to innovation investment and to end the "boom and bust" nature of the company's innovation efforts (see "The balanced venture porfolio" on page 37). Traditionally, he points out, the company has seen its level of innovative activity cycle every 10 years, as low growth prompts calls for extra innovation, only for an activity peak to be followed by a period of consolidation during which some of the best innovators may leave.

To co-ordinate these efforts, DSM has set up an Innovation Centre encompassing the CTO's office; a business incubator; an "innovation shared service centre" (the nexus of the company's open innovation programme, managing licensing, venturing and IPR management); and EBA project teams, each steered by the EBA director, the chief innovation officer and representatives from relevant business groups.

The journey of a great idea

Any scientist or engineer on DSM's staff can submit an idea to the company's Innovation Centre using a one-page form on the company intranet. Their submission will then be checked for strategic fit and commercial attractiveness based on 19 criteria. "We look more at the fit than the attractiveness, at this stage," Mr Kirschbaum says. If the Centre approves the idea, and if the first phase of its R&D will cost less than €50k, then the innovator is given the budget and the freedom to proceed.

If, after this phase, the idea is good enough, then it could be transferred straight to an operating unit for rapid commercial deployment. In most cases, however, it will need further R&D and test marketing. To become a true venture, it must pass through several "gates". At the first, it must show "attractiveness" and "fit" with the DSM competences and pass a basic SWOT analysis. At the second, it must demonstrate its value in a "5Cs" analysis – context, customers, competitors, company, costs – and the proof of concept must be available. At the third, it must have a marketing plan that satisfies a "5P" analysis – product, promotion, personal selling, price, place. At any point, a project may be stopped, and the technology may be offered to other parties via licensing. Equally, Mr Kirschbaum points out, if another party has a similar project at a similar stage of development, it could be cost-effective to acquire or license that rather than persist with the internal innovation.

DSM views its innovation funnel as a cyclone, absorbing and ejecting technologies

Overall, DSM views its innovation funnel as a "cyclone" stimulated by licensing agreements, that can absorb or eject technologies as needed.

The bullet-proof material with hidden strengths

Dyneema® is a synthetic fibre 15 times stronger than steel. Based on a specialty polyethylene (the material commonly used to make the underside surface of skis), it was invented by DSM in 1979, entered commercial production in 1990 and has since become one of the company's most valuable brands. It has so many applications – ranging from bullet-proof fabrics to ropes, cables and nets to surgical sutures – that DSM has set up a dedicated office to solicit new ones from interested third-parties.

"The inventor was a friend of mine, who produced a small piece of the fibre and patented it," Mr Kirschbaum says. "He told me that to build a pilot line he needed an engineer who was stupid enough to try to wind a bobbin of the stuff, which was really, really difficult – in this state, the fibre would be at its weakest. Preventing breakage was therefore the challenge." The year was 1982, DSM had just posted its first loss in 80 years and it had little fibre experience. Yet Mr Kirschbaum managed to persuade the board that the idea was worth pursuing. The board merely insisted that he find an external partner to help develop it. "I would call that extrapreneurship," he says, "going outside to find moral and financial support to get done within the company what you think is good." (For a full definition of extrapreneurship, see page 54).

Dyneema needed an extrapreneur to seek out moral and financial support externally

During his search for a partner, Mr Kirschbaum had to overcome not only the technical difficulties of spinning such an exotic material but also an IP battle with a US company that believed (mistakenly) that Dyneema® infringed its patents. Ironically, it was the lump-sum settlement paid by this challenger that eventually enabled DSM to forge a joint venture with a Japanese company to develop Dyneema® into a viable product. "If such a breakthrough invention arose today, all the scientist would have to do is contact the Innovation Centre, to get the innovation process started," Mr Kirschbaum points out.

Open Innovation in Action

3.5 Tate & Lyle

Summary

● Tate & Lyle is using open innovation to help shift its focus from commodities to value-added products and services.

● The company still acts as a traditional ingredients supplier, but increasingly it is marketing packaged solutions to customers, based on its own research into end-consumer preferences.

● It has set up a venture fund, Tate & Lyle Ventures, to invest in start-ups and expansion-stage companies. This fund will leverage the expertise of Tate & Lyle to enhance the value of its portfolio. It will also improve Tate & Lyle's knowledge of emerging technologies.

Tate & Lyle was established in 1921 with the merger of two sugar refiners, and its core business changed very little until the 1980s, when it invested in starch in the US and Europe. Today, the company calls itself a "food and industrial ingredients manufacturer" and has declared an intention to become "the world's leading renewable ingredients business." In the search for higher margins, it has shifted its focus from supply to demand.

In the run-up to the Millennium, Tate & Lyle sensed, like many other commodity-based businesses in the West, that it would have to move up the value chain if it wanted to carry on growing. It had to continue to leverage its refining capabilities and expertise; and create more value-added products such as specialty sweeteners and functional ingredients for food and industrial products. To this end, it divested about 30 businesses regarded as non-core before, in 2003, recruiting a new CEO, Iain Ferguson, to deliver a fresh, transformative vision for the long-term.

Tate & Lyle has shifted its focus from basic ingredients to value-added solutions

Staff rallied around the new strategy thanks to 300 workshops held in 40 countries

Mr Ferguson had previously been senior vice-president of corporate development at Unilever, where he'd championed the introduction of open innovation. Accordingly, when he approved a new mission statement for Tate & Lyle, it echoed the principles of openness, collaboration and market-sensitivity described in Parts I and II of this book: "We will grow by uniting our businesses and developing partnerships to create the world's leading renewable ingredients business. We will build a consistent global portfolio of distinctive, profitable, high-value solutions in products and services for our customers."

Mr Ferguson realised he would need the support of all Tate & Lyle's stakeholders – employees, customers, shareholders, partners, suppliers and the communities in which Tate & Lyle's big facilities played a major role. So he initiated a campaign in 2004 called "Vision into Action", involving 300 workshops with 6,000 employees in over 40 countries and 12 languages. "To sustain the momentum we've since used regular line-management presentations, management committee presentations, and a roadshow of what people are doing to fulfil the new strategy, involving 'vision booths' and staff vox pops," Mr Ferguson says, adding that "one of the things that keeps corporate cynicism at bay is success; we've doubled the share price since the programme started."

Moving up the value chain

Although 80% of Tate & Lyle's sales volume still comes from its commodity business, half its profit now comes from value-added products and the group is looking to increase this further. "Increasingly we look at our business as one that serves end markets," Mr Ferguson says. "Ninety per cent of what we do is still business-to-business, but it's good to have a stake in the consumer side because talking directly to the consumer gives us a good insight into trends. We're an asset-heavy business but one that responds increasingly well to signals from the market."

Tate & Lyle has been running a consumer research programme in Europe and the Americas since 2004, to gather "qualitative and quantitative data on people's dietary habits, lifestyles and health aspirations." The aim of this process is to "help [its] customers lead in the marketplace." In other words,

Tate & Lyle is no longer pitching new products to its business-to-business customers without considering the market context for those products (see "The open innovation bow-tie" on page 25). This approach has two major benefits: (i) it helps Tate & Lyle to focus its R&D resources on innovations for which market demand is high; and (ii) it helps Tate & Lyle to position itself as a service provider that can help customers to launch innovative new products of their own.

The company uses the acronym CORE™ to describe the "solution sets" it can provide, as follows:

- **CREATE**™. "Innovations in shape, structure, taste and texture – helping make our customers' products even more exciting and distinctive."

- **OPTIMIZE**™. "Maximising efficiency and added-value services – helping our customers meet their cost and margin targets."

- **REBALANCE**™. "Reformulating to lower fat, lower sugar and lower calorie positions without compromising on taste."

- **ENRICH**™. "Enhancing the nutritional benefits of products without compromising on taste."

Changing R&D priorities

Tate & Lyle is spending more than ever on its R&D function: around $37m in the 2006 financial year, compared with $24m in 2002. It also increased its R&D headcount over the same period from 150 to 230. And, like other companies trying to embrace open innovation, it is devoting an increasing proportion of this spend to the gathering of knowledge from external sources. It has a target of spending 4-5% of value-added turnover on R&D, which breaks down as follows:

Application/product development	47%
Fundamental research in-house	24%
Alliances with academic institutions	12%
Ventures	12%
Process improvement	5%

Tate & Lyle chooses which innovations to develop internally based on a net-present value assessment, and an iterative R&D process based on an innovation funnel system. As far as its university collaboration is concerned, it invests in institutions that have highly specialised research facilities and has recently announced cooperations with Kings College in London and with the Industrial Platform of the Kluyver Centre for Genomics of Industrial Fermentation in Holland. It invests in specific research projects based on whether they are likely to be cost-effective in comparison with the in-house alternative. "University patent management is getting tougher though," Mr Ferguson concedes. "Twenty years ago, universities were happy to get the research money, now your second conversation with any university is with its IP manager."

The company's long-term innovation planning is based on a portfolio approach (see "The balanced venture portfolio" on page 37). In 2006, it launched a venture fund, Tate & Lyle Ventures, which will invest up to $45m "in start-ups and expansion-stage companies that support Tate & Lyle's strategic focus." Like any other VC fund, it will be judged chiefly on the financial returns it produces. It should be able to make better investment decisions, and advise the companies in its portfolio more effectively, by leveraging Tate & Lyle's expertise. It should also be able to keep Tate & Lyle's core R&D function apprised of new technologies. Ultimately, it should provide options in likely areas of "technology push", in the same way that consumer research is already helping Tate & Lyle to focus on likely areas of "market pull".

This strategy that will depend on independence, Mr Ferguson says: "I think smart money finds smart ideas, and I think smart entrepreneurs find smart money. I want to give them even more insulation from Tate & Lyle in the longer term by bringing in other investors. The fund, which is registered with the FSA, is in discussions with a select number of financial institutions with a view to raising additional finance."

A sweet success story

Tate & Lyle's flagship success story, in terms of both partnering and sales growth, is SPLENDA® Sucralose. The smash-hit no-calorie sweetener was discovered way back in 1976, but even then its success owed a lot to open innovation principles. It was discovered by a Tate & Lyle scientist collaborating with researchers at Queen Elizabeth College, now part of King's College London. The research student was discussing his work with his supervisor on the telephone, misheard the instruction to "test it" and tasted it instead. Its sweetness turned out to be approximately six hundred times greater than that of sugar, even though it doesn't contain any calories.

Tate & Lyle's Ventures fund will effectively buy options in emergent technologies

Tate & Lyle formed an alliance with McNeil Nutritionals, a subsidiary of Johnson & Johnson, to develop sucralose into a product, and later to share responsibility for its production and marketing. However, when Mr Ferguson took over, he realised the deal was no longer serving the best interests of either party. In line with open innovation principles, each needed to concentrate on what it did best. "We were seeing an explosion of demand with the popularity and realised we needed much more capacity. In effect, we needed to treat SPLENDA® Sucralose as a kind of FMCG," Mr Ferguson says. The alliance was thus realigned so that McNeil retained ownership of the SPLENDA® brand, with commercial responsibility for its retail and food service businesses, while Tate & Lyle became the sole manufacturer, responsible for global sales to food and beverage manufacturers. SPLENDA® is now an ingredient in over 4,000 products, and accounted for 21% of Tate & Lyle's EBITA in the year to 31 March 2006.

To conclude, Tate & Lyle is actively using open innovation as part of a coherent strategy to continue the transformation of the business, maintaining its success in creating added-value solutions and increasing its return to shareholders.

SPLENDA® is trademark of McNeil Nutritionals, LLC

References

1 "Knowledge Transfer through Inheritance: Spin-out Generation, Development and Performance," by Rajshree Agarwal, Raj Echambadi, April Franco, MB Sarkar, Raj Echambadi, April Franco and MB Sarkar, Academy of Management Journal 2004, 47(4): 501-522.

2 *Open Innovation: The New Imperative for Creating and Profiting from Technology,* by Henry Chesbrough; Harvard Business School Press (2003).

3 "Mind to Market: A Global Analysis of University Biotechnology Transfer and Commercialisation," by Ross DeVol and Armen Bedroussian; The Milken Institute (September 2006).

4 *The Growth Gamble: When Leaders Should Bet Big on New Business, and How They Can Avoid Expensive Failures,* by Andrew Campbell and Robert Park; Nicholas Brealey Publications (2005).

5 *Winning Ideas for Strategic Growth and Venturing,* by Andrew Gaule and Andy Morrison; H-I Network (2005).

6 *Intrapreneuring: Why You Don't Have to Leave the Corporation to Become an Entrepreneur,* by Gifford Pinchot; Harper & Row (1985).

Further reading

● *Innovation Performance Measurement: Striking the Right Balance,* by David Birchall, George Tovstiga, Andy Morrison and Andrew Gaule; H-I Network (2004).

● *Review of Leading Global Corporate Venturing Units,* by Andrew Gaule and Maura Moore; H-I Network (2004).

● *Going Beyond the Idea: Delivering Successful Corporate Innovation,* by Andy Morrison; H-I Network (2003).

● *Innovation Leadership: Roles and Key Imperatives,* by Jill Hender; H-I Network (2003).

● *Corporate Venturing: Rewarding Entrepreneurial Talent,* by Andrew Gaule and Nigel Spinks; H-I Network (2002).